LITIGATING MORALITY

Litigating Morality

AMERICAN LEGAL THOUGHT
AND ITS ENGLISH
ROOTS

Wayne C. Bartee
Alice Fleetwood Bartee

PRAEGER

New York
Westport, Connecticut
London

Library of Congress Cataloging-in-Publication Data

Bartee, Wayne C.
    Litigating morality : American legal thought and its English roots
    Wayne C. Bartee, Alice Fleetwood Bartee.
      p.   cm.
    Includes index.
    ISBN 0-275-94127-2 (alk. paper)
    1. Sex and law—United States—History. 2. Insanity—
Jurisprudence—United States—History. 3. Punishment—United
States—History. 4. Sex and law—Great Britain—History.
5. Insanity—Jurisprudence—Great Britain—History. 6. Punishment—
Great Britain—History. 7. Law and ethics. I. Bartee, Alice Fleetwood.
II. Title.
K5194.B37   1992
170—dc20   91-27816

British Library Cataloguing in Publication Data is available.

Library of Congress Catalog Card Number: 91-27816
ISBN: 0-275-94127-2

First published in 1992

Praeger Publishers, One Madison Avenue, New York, NY 10010
An imprint of Greenwood Publishing Group, Inc.

Printed in the United States of America

The paper used in this book complies with the
Permanent Paper Standard issued by the National
Information Standards Organization (Z39.48-1984).

10 9 8 7 6 5 4 3 2 1

This book is dedicated to our sons,
Clark and Fleetwood

Contents

Acknowledgments

The authors wish to express our appreciation to the secretarial staffs of the Department of Political Science, the Department of Philosophy, and the Department of History of Southwest Missouri State University for their efficient assistance with this manuscript. We are particularly grateful, also, to the reference librarians of the university for their generous help. A. F. Bartee especially acknowledges her long-standing intellectual debt to Professor Judith Jarvis Thomson's analytic philosophy class at Barnard College, Columbia University.

Introduction

Americans have a propensity for settling disputes within a legal framework. The aims of litigants have varied widely from the noblest to the most sordid, yet they have found in the legal process an appropriate method for debating and resolving issues ranging from the mundane to the most bizarre. This has indeed proved to be the case with issues identified as moral in nature. At times defined as conformity to accepted social customs of right behavior, the term "moral" has been interpreted expansively. Sometimes morality has been associated with sexual conduct defined as virtuous; at other times it has related to values such as honesty, integrity, and truthfulness. Often morality has been linked with religion and distinguished from mere civic or legal righteousness; it has implied a higher, nobler level of behavior.[1] Numerous and diverse types of behavior have been evaluated according to morality standards. Issues associated with sexual behavior such as abortion, sodomy, and pornography are regularly debated as moral issues. In addition, society's treatment of those who fail to conform to its chosen standards of behavior has raised moral questions. Thus appropriate punishment for criminals has become a debatable moral issue, particularly when society deals with offenders who may be insane. Punishment itself has also become a moral issue as society has debated its basic nature and forms.

Litigating morality is not a recent phenomenon; neither is it uniquely American. It is an inherited approach rooted in centuries-old English traditions and practices and incorporated into the American colonial experience. Colonial Americans, like their English forebears, used law and legal actions to define and record their moral values. Modern-day Americans have inherited from the English legal culture an extensive record of litigation of moral issues. The legal process that has documented this litigation includes numerous elements that have individually and collectively influenced the course of moral disputes. Among these are written laws which either in statutory form or in constitutional documents record past moral choices; judges and juries who apply and interpret these laws along with established precedents; and the legal scholars and attorneys who have the job of explaining, defending, and at times of challenging earlier moral choices. The linking of these elements of the legal process with the evolution of significant moral issues can provide a unique framework for analysis of the process and of litigating morality in America. Such is the purpose of this book.

The English roots of American legal thought clearly document historical traditions as sources of values. This does not mean, as some constitutional authorities[2] have inferred, that fundamental rights extracted from these historical traditions will be inherently limited and conservative ones. Historical sources seldom condense into a single judgment: these English roots are susceptible to interpretation. As such, they are not the property of any one ideological group. Thus analysis of the litigation of moral issues demonstrates that liberals and conservatives alike appeal to English traditions to justify their moral positions.

The morality of abortion and the role of legal scholars in identifying and elaborating society's choices is the subject of Chapter 1, "English Legal Scholars and Abortion in American Law." Legal and moral opinions on the abortion issue have been handed down in the works of the great English common law scholars from Bracton through Blackstone and are incorporated into American case precedents like *Roe v. Wade* (1973)[3] and *Webster v. Reproductive Health Services* (1989)[4]. These opinions permeate the intellectual debate advanced by both pro-life and pro-choice advocates.

In Chapter 2, "English Common and Statutory Law and Sodomy in American Law," the debate over gay rights is analyzed by linking English sodomy statutes and legal customs with U.S. court decisions and legislative policies. Thus "The Trial of the Earl of Castlehaven for Sodomy" (1628) has impacted the 1986 U.S. Supreme Court decision, *Bowers v. Hardwick*[5] and influenced the status of gay rights in America. The limiting nature of historical English traditions on fundamental rights is most evident here. Yet, here also, alternate historical traditions provide support for increased personal privacy.

Pornography, like sodomy and abortion, also presents a moral question which has perplexed the legal system for centuries. Chapter 3, "Pornography: English Precedents in American Legal Thought," identifies the judicial tests for pornography developed by English judges and modified by their American counterparts. These tests demonstrate the role of judges in defining pornography. Their criteria is explored in part through a case study of the notorious novel, *Memoirs of a Woman of Pleasure* (Fanny Hill), written in 1748 and prosecuted until 1966 on both sides of the Atlantic.

Chapter 4, "The Criminal Insanity Defense: English and American Attorneys," deals with society's struggle to balance leniency toward the insane with punishment for their criminal acts. A central aspect of this moral struggle is that of defining insanity. Deciding how to treat the criminally insane forces society to confront its darker side, namely, its attitude toward weaker members. Legal history documents the crucial role played by early English and American attorneys in defining insanity. As attorneys introduced the expert witness and suggested new tests for insanity, they created a body of case law central to litigation of this moral issue. Their litigation tactics from early English cases like *Regina v. Daniel McNaughton* (1843)[6] to American examples like *United States v. John Hinckley* (1982)[7] demonstrate the legal process at work.

Finally, the debates over the morality of punishments—particularly the death penalty—have focused attention on the meaning of the Eighth Amendment to the U.S. Constitution. Tied to the English Bill of Rights of 1689 by both language and history, the Eighth Amendment prohibits punishments that are excessive, cruel, and unusual. Applying this standard has been a continuing task for judges and justices. The legal thought that links English constitutional documents like Magna Carta and the English Bill of Rights with the U.S. Constitution identifies the various standards used to determine appropriate penalties. These emerge in Chapter 5, "English Constitutional Documents and Punishment in American Law," and are documented in cases from *Titus Oates* (1685)[8] in seventeenth-century England to *Solem v. Helm* (1983)[9] in twentieth-century America. Liberals and conservatives alike have found in historical traditions arguments appropriate for their position on the moral question of the death penalty.

All of these moral issues share a common attribute: they trigger deep and intense emotional responses which are not based on economic goals.[10] They are issues that do not lend themselves to compromise but instead engender irreconcilable conflict. And it is the litigation process that has been identified by society—past and present—as the appropriate framework for managing these continuing controversies.

NOTES

1. *Webster's Unabridged New International Dictionary*, 3rd ed., s.v. "morality."

2. Laurence Tribe and Michael Dorf, *On Reading the Constitution* (Cambridge, MA: Harvard University Press, 1991), pp. 98–101.

3. 410 U.S. 111 (1973).

4. 492 U.S. 490 (1989).

5. 478 U.S. 186 (1986).

6. Regina v. McNaughton, T. B. Howell (ed.), *State Trials* (London: New Series, 1843) vol. 4, p. 847.

7. 672 F. 2c. 115 (D.C. cir.).

8. Rex v. Titus Oates, T. B. Howell (ed.), *State Trials*, vol. 10, p. 1,079.

9. 463 U.S. 277 (1983).

10. Raymond Tatalovich and Byron Daynes (eds.), *Social Regulatory Policy: Moral Controversies in American Politics* (Boulder, CO: Westview Press, 1988), p. 211.

LITIGATING MORALITY

Chapter 1 —————————————————————————

English Legal Scholars and Abortion in American Law

English legal scholars are well-known actors on the American judicial stage. The names of Blackstone and Coke, familiar to attorneys and judges in eighteenth-century America, are still cited by Americans in the twentieth century. Their scholarly legal treatises, detailing ancient English cases and offering the writer's analysis, have long been standard acquisitions of U.S. libraries. From the writings of Bracton in the thirteenth century through those of Blackstone in the eighteenth century, Americans have drawn legal doctrines and standards and have applied them to American issues. Protagonists in the bitter moral and legal controversy over abortion in America have sought to fortify their positions with the views of these prominent English legal authorities. Since all of these ancient scholars dealt with the abortion issue over the centuries in England, there is substantial material available, particularly for the sixteenth, seventeenth, and eighteenth centuries. Moreover, the central question in the contemporary abortion debate was also that of these earlier periods, namely, "At what point—if any—does the abortion of a fetus become a crime?"

The relevance of English legal scholars for answering this question emerged in two landmark abortion cases in America: *Roe v. Wade*, 410 U.S. 113 (1973) and *Webster v. Reproductive Health Services*, 492 U.S. 490 (1989). In each case the oral arguments, the written briefs, and the judicial opinions demonstrated how each side in the abortion debate bolstered its position through appeals to the great scholars of the English common law tradition—Bracton, Coke, Hale, and Blackstone. *Roe v. Wade*, the first major abortion case to be decided by the U.S. Supreme Court, had included an extensive discussion of the positions on abortion

taken by English legal scholars. The author of the *Roe* opinion, Mr.
Justice Harry J. Blackmun, had originally intended to base his opinion
primarily on this historical argument, and was only persuaded later by
Justice William J. Brennan, Jr., to include the section highlighting privacy rights.[1] The debate over the views of English legal scholars nevertheless continued to influence Justice Blackmun, and he devoted the first
part of his opinion in *Roe* to an analysis of the abortion positions taken
by English common law scholars. Any major court challenge seeking to
overturn the *Roe* decision needed to address this section, therefore, and
to persuade the Court to reevaluate its interpretation of these English
roots. Such was the aim in *Webster* in 1989 where oral arguments and
briefs raised these issues again. Thus the English roots of American legal
thought on abortion emerged in *Roe* and reemerged in *Webster* to demonstrate their relevance in the litigation of this highly emotional moral
issue.

WEBSTER, ROE, AND ENGLISH LEGAL SCHOLARS

In April 1989, a Missouri abortion clinic known as Reproductive
Health Services found itself in court arguing against a Missouri state law
that imposed extensive regulations on abortions. Mr. Frank Susman, a
veteran pro-choice attorney, had been chosen to represent the clinic in
oral argument before the U.S. Supreme Court. The Court's membership
at that time included two justices who had never confronted the abortion
issue—Justices Anthony Kennedy and Antonin Scalia. Both engaged in
extensive dialogue with counsel during the oral argument: Justice Scalia
raised and debated the historic abortion position taken by the ancient
English common law scholars. Mr. Susman opened the door for these
questions when he argued that before the year 1820 abortion had not
been regulated in America and insisted that "abortion" was accepted, it
was not a crime at common law as *Roe v. Wade* and other works have
recognized."[2] Justice Scalia responded immediately, "That certainly is
not uncontested."[3] The justice then pointed out that two historical briefs
had been filed in the *Webster* case and that one of these presented a view
contradictory to that asserted by the counsel for Reproductive Health
Services. Justice Scalia continued, "The Association for Public Justice . . .
quotes authorities back to Blackstone and Coke saying that at common
law abortion was unlawful."[4] This particular brief had been written to
challenge the interpretation of English common law scholars accepted
by the U.S. Supreme Court in 1973 in *Roe v. Wade* in which the Court
had held that the majority of early English legal scholars had not defined
abortion as a crime.

Closely tied to the question of English legal scholars' positions on
abortion was the issue of a dividing line or point to separate legal from

illegal abortions. This point was called "quickening" by the early authorities. Questions about this line were also raised in oral argument in *Webster*: Justice Anthony Kennedy asked counsel for the Reproductive Health Clinic if states had the right to "prohibit an abortion after the fetus is eight months old."[5] Mr. Susman's response went immediately to the old issue of the dividing line between legal and illegal abortions. "I am willing to recognize the compelling interest granted in *Roe* of the state in potential fetal life after the point of viability," Susman responded. He then linked the ancient concept of "quickening" as the dividing line to that of the modern viability standard.

There are many cogent reasons for picking the point of viability [as the dividing line for state regulations] which is what we have today under *Roe*. [H]istorically, both at common law and in early statutes, *this was always the line chosen. Whether it was called quickening or viability, there is little difference time wise.*[6]

Justice Sandra Day O'Connor, demanding clarification of the quickening line, asked if it had to do with the time at which the woman first detected movement of the fetus. Mr. Susman agreed, noting that quickening occurred two or three weeks before what *Roe* had defined as viability, or the point at which a fetus could live outside the mother. Justice Kennedy's concern that courts should not engage in "line-drawing" as it had in *Roe* was a needless one, Mr. Susman insisted, because early English legal scholars and courts had done this with quickening.

Thus *Webster* raised again the role of English common law authorities and precedents in defining the abortion debate's issues. Positions of these scholars and their standards, deemed settled in *Roe*, were once again argued. The different interpretations possible can be understood first by evaluating the reasoning by which the Supreme Court in 1973 in *Roe* concluded that English legal scholars had not defined abortion of even a quick fetus as a crime. Second, a focus on the new interpretation advanced in briefs and oral arguments in *Webster* in 1989 identifies the reasoning used to link Blackstone and Coke to criminalization of abortion. Finally, analysis of the ancient legal authorities from Bracton to Blackstone establishes the frame of reference used in both of these court cases to reach different conclusions about the English roots of abortion rights in American legal thought.

ROE V. WADE: THE ROLE OF ENGLISH LEGAL SCHOLARS IN COURT OPINION AND ORAL ARGUMENT

The written opinion of the U.S. Supreme Court in the 1973 landmark abortion case of *Roe v. Wade* stated that the majority sought to resolve the abortion issue in part by using "what history reveals about society's attitude toward the abortion procedure over the centuries."[7] At stake in *Roe* was the legality of a Texas statute prohibiting abortion unless the mother's life was endangered. Early in the opinion the Court explained the impact which historical English judicial decisions on abortion and the opinion of prominent English legal scholars had on their decision. This part of the Court's opinion in *Roe v. Wade* focused on three major variables: the status of abortion under early English common law; the views and opinions of the "common lawyers" including Bracton, Coke, and Blackstone; and the impact of English authorities—judicial and legislative—on early American legislative and judicial decisions dealing with abortion. Based on this review of legal history, the U.S. Supreme Court in *Roe v. Wade* reached the conclusion that modern abortion laws of the late nineteenth and early twentieth centuries were "aberrations inconsistent with the earlier English doctrines and American practices."[8] Concluding that early English judicial opinions had created a body of common law that dealt "leniently" with abortion, the Court balanced "lessons [from] medical and legal history with the lenity of the common law, and with the demands of the profound problems of the present day."[9] This balancing contributed to the judicial decision in *Roe v. Wade*. The Court's analysis of the English common law's treatment of abortion used the works of Bracton, Coke, and Blackstone in the text of the opinion and supplemented this with the additional names of Hawkins and Hale in the footnotes. The relevance of these great common law scholars for the Court is documented in the following section:

ROE v. WADE (excerpt)

[We] feel it desirable briefly to survey, in several aspects, the history of abortion, for such insight as that history may afford us, and then to examine the state purposes and interests behind the criminal abortion laws.(...)

It perhaps is not generally appreciated that the restrictive criminal abortion laws in effect in a majority of States today are of relatively recent vintage. Those laws, generally proscribing abortion or its attempt at any time during pregnancy except when necessary to preserve the pregnant woman's life, are not of ancient or even of common-law origin. Instead, they derive from statutory changes effected, for the most part, in the latter half of the 19th century.(...)

The common law. It is undisputed that at common law, abortion performed *before* "quickening"—the first recognizable movement of the fetus *in utero*, appearing usually from the 16th to the 18th week of pregnancy[a]—was not

[a](...)

an indictable offense.[b] The absence of a common-law crime for pre-quickening abortion appears to have developed from a confluence of earlier philosophical, theological, and civil and canon law concepts of when life begins. . . .[c] Bracton focused upon quickening as the critical point. The significance of quickening was echoed by later common-law scholars and found its way into the received common-law in this country.

Whether abortion of a *quick* fetus was a felony at common law, or even a lesser crime, is still disputed. Bracton, writing early in the thirteenth century, thought it homicide.[d] But the later and predominant view, following the great common-law scholars, has been that it was, at most, a lesser offense. In a frequently cited passage, Coke took the position that abortion of a woman "quick with childe" is "a great misprision, and no murder."[e] Blackstone followed, saying that while abortion after quickening had once been considered manslaughter (though not murder), "modern law" took a less severe view.[f] A recent review of the common-law precedents argues, however, that those precedents contradict Coke and that even post-quickening abortion was never established as a common-law crime.[g] This

[b] E. Coke, Institutes III* 50; 1 W. Hawkins, Pleas of the Crown, c. 31:16 (4th ed. 1762); 1 W. Blackstone, Commentaries* 129–130; M. Hale, Pleas of the Crown 433 (1st Amer. ed. 1847). For discussions of the role of the quickening concept in English common law, see Lader 78; Noonan 223–226; Means, The Law of New York Concerning Abortion and the Status of the Foetus, 1664–1968: A Case of Cessation of Constitutionality (pt. 1), 14 N.Y.L.F. 411, 418–428 (1968) (hereinafter Means I).(. . .)

[c] (. . .) See Means I, pp. 411–412. . . .

[d] Bracton took the position that abortion by blow or poison was homicide "if the foetus be already formed and animated, and particularly if it be animated." 2 II. Bracton, De Legibus et Consuetudinibus Angliae 279 (T. Twiss ed. 1879), or, as a later translation puts it, "if the foetus is already formed or quickened, especially if it is quickened." 2 II. Bracton, On the Laws and Customs of England 341 (S. Thorne ed. 1968). See Quay 431; see also 2 Fleta 60–61 (Book 1, c. 23) (Selden Society ed. 1955).

[e] E. Coke, Institutes III* 50.

[f] I. W. Blackstone, Commentaries* 129–130.

[g] Means, The Phoenix of Abortional Freedom: Is a Penumbral or Ninth-Amendment Right About to Arise from the Nineteenth-Century Legislative Ashes of a Fourteenth-Century Common-Law Liberty?, 17 N.Y.L.F. 335 (1971) (hereinafter Means II). The author examines the two principal precedents cited marginally by Coke, both contrary to his dictum, and traces the treatment of these and other cases by earlier commentators. He concludes that Coke, who himself participated as an advocate in an abortion case in 1601, may have intentionally misstated the law. The author even suggests a reason: Coke's strong feelings against abortion, coupled with his determination to assert common-law (secular) jurisdiction to assess penalties for an offense that traditionally had been an exclusively ecclesiastical or canon-law crime. See also Lader 78–79, who notes that some scholars doubt that the common law ever was applied to abortion; that the English ecclesiastical courts seem to have lost interest in the problem after 1527 and that the preamble to the English legislation of 1803, 43 Geo. 3, c. 58, section 1, referred to in the text, *infra*, at 718, states that "no adequate means have been hitherto provided for the prevention and punishment of such offenses."

is of some importance because while most American courts ruled, in holding or dictum, that abortion of an unquickened fetus was not criminal
under their received common law, others followed Coke in stating that
abortion of a quick fetus was a "misprision," a term they translated to mean
"misdemeanor." That their reliance on Coke on this aspect of the law as
uncritical and, apparently in all the reported cases, dictum (due probably
to the paucity of common-law prosecutions for post-quickening abortion),
makes it now appear doubtful that abortion was ever firmly established as
a common-law crime even with respect to the destruction of a quick fetus.

Oral argument in *Roe v. Wade* had highlighted the questions about
the English common law's decisions concerning abortion. Briefs submitted by both parties to the case were supplemented by *amici curiae*
briefs and these provided the framework for the oral argument. Attorneys for both sides in the argument and reargument discussed abortion
in English common law precedents and the legal relationship between
the age-old concept of quickening and that of criminal abortion. Ms.
Sara Weddington, attorney for Jane Roe, distributed to all members of
the Court and to opposing counsel copies of an article written by Professor Cyril Means, Jr., of the New York University Law School. This
article reanalyzed English common law scholarship in the period between
Bracton and Coke. Throughout Ms. Weddington's oral presentation she
referred often to this article. Her original brief also contained a summary
and analysis of the available data on the common law, abortion, and
quickening. She argued that,

At common law, abortion could be induced by a physician, midwife, or anyone
without penalty, prior to the period of pregnancy called "quickening".... This
principle was accepted in the overwhelming majority of American jurisdictions.
From 1828 onward, however, states began to modify the common law rule by
legislation which prohibited forms of abortion at all stages of pregnancy.[10]

Ms. Weddington's brief urged the court to return the country to the
common law rules that had governed abortion originally and to permit
abortions, thus "preserve[ing] ... the 117-year-old *purpose* [intent] of the
[Texas] law, and the common law."[11] During her oral argument Ms.
Weddington also highlighted two early common law abortion cases: the
so-called *Twinslayer's Case* (1327) and the *Abortionist's Case* (1348). These
two case precedents seemed to uphold the theory that in early English
common law, abortion at *any* stage of gestation was not a felony. Ms.
Weddington urged the court to recognize that "at the time the Constitution was adopted" in America there was "no common law prohibition
against abortion; ... they were available to the women of this country."[12]

Opposing counsel for the states of Texas and Georgia tried to convince
the U.S. Supreme Court that common law precedent had regarded abor-

tion as an evil act and sometimes criminal. Their arguments repeated these points made by attorneys representing the National Right to Life Committee and filed in a brief *amicus curiae* by this group. It included the following statement:

From Bracton's day abortion was regarded at common law as a serious evil or wrong which should be prevented. . . . For a brief period, difficulties of proving that abortion had in fact caused the termination of an "unquick" child prevented application of the serious sanctions of the criminal law to some cases.[13]

This brief, then, claimed that Bracton defined "abortion" as homicide if the fetus were "formed and especially if it were ensouled," and that Coke repeated Bracton, stating that an abortion of a woman "quick with child" was a great misprision and *so* murder."[14] These attorneys suggested to the court that Coke's use of the "quickening" criteria might have been "erroneously imposed" and they thought that abortion at any stage really had been a felony originally. During the oral argument, Mr. Robert Flowers, assistant attorney general for the state of Texas, argued that "Blackstone observed . . . that life is inherent by nature in every individual and exists even before the child is born." The Court responded with the question: "Mr. Flowers, when you quote Blackstone, is it not true that in Blackstone's time abortion was not a felony?" Assistant Attorney General Flowers then suggested that the framers of the U.S. Constitution *thought* that abortion was a crime at common law even though it actually was not.[15] The attorney general of the state of Georgia presented a written brief in *Roe*'s companion case, *Doe v. Bolton*, 410 U.S. 179 (1973), which made a major issue of the fact that Georgia's Constitution had incorporated the English common law in 1784. He maintained that English common law criminalized abortion, and asked the Court to uphold modern anti-abortion statutes on that basis.[16]

Extensive content footnotes, citations, and references cited by the U.S. Supreme Court in *Roe v. Wade* demonstrated concern for properly defining the status of abortion under this body of early English common law. This was apparently deemed necessary in order to properly assess the claim made by the attorneys general of Texas and Georgia. Thus the *Roe* Court majority evaluated the English common law scholars including Henry de Bracton's *On the Laws and Customs of England*, Coke's *Institutes*, and Blackstone's *Commentaries*. They also examined the works of William Hawkins and Sir Matthew Hale. The judicial majority on the basis of this research apparently reached the conclusion that Bracton's view defining abortion of an "ensouled" fetus as murder was not the "dominant" view of the time. Bracton, the Court decided, had simply stated what he "thought" as opposed to what the case precedents actually demonstrated about the status of abortion at common law. These justices also decided to interpret Bracton's "ensoulment" as being the equivalent of quickening. In addition, the *Roe* Court's seven-man majority opinion distinguished Bracton from the "great common law scholars" and noted that Coke and Blackstone had held that abortion of a quick fetus was a "misprision" only and *not* murder. The Court thus set aside Bracton as a valid common law authority for establishing abortion as a crime. An examination of Coke and Blackstone and other common law scholars and judges, however, led the Court to the two fourteenth-century common law case precedents—the *Twinslayer's Case* (1327) and the *Abortionist's Case* (1348)—and to Hale's treatises which discussed these cases. The *Roe* majority reached the conclusion that these two common law precedents actually contradicted Coke's statement that post-quickened abortion was a "misprision." The Court thus accepted the thesis that Coke's categorization of post-quickened abortion as "misprision" was his own invention, independent of the existing current theory or practice. Coke did this, they concluded, to make abortion into a crime cognizable by the court over which he himself presided. Coke's struggle with the jurisdiction asserted by church courts and his own personal intense dislike of abortion were thus highlighted by the *Roe* Court majority.

The holding ultimately set forth by the U.S. Supreme Court in 1973 in *Roe v. Wade* concluded that early English common law authorities had not defined abortion as a crime. In fact, the Court claimed, "It is thus apparent that at common law, at the time of the adoption of our Constitution, and throughout the major portion of the 19th century,...a woman enjoyed a [broad] right to [abortion]...." However, the Court noted that the "lenity of the common law" had to be balanced against the "demands of the profound problems of the present day." Thus *Roe* concluded with a recognition of state power to "place increasing restrictions on abortion" particularly after the "compelling point [of] viability" had been reached.[17]

DEBATING *ROE'S* INTERPRETATION OF ENGLISH LEGALISTS: WEBSTER

"*Roe v. Wade* was based upon erroneous notions of the historical status of abortion under the common law and [is] a sharp break with long established traditions and values embodied in the common law and our Constitution."[18] This was the position taken by lawyers and scholars affiliated with two pro-life groups who filed briefs in the *Webster* case. They urged the Court to reexamine the writings of English legal scholars and they offered new interpretations. Arguing that Bracton's view of "abortion after quickening [as] a criminal homicide" was the established view before 1500, the pro-life scholars reevaluated the two early English case precedents known as the *Twinslayer's Case* (1327) and the *Abortionist's*

Case (1348). They suggested to the Court that the prosecution for abortion in each case had failed due to early procedural technicalities and problems of evidence rather than because abortion was not a crime. This new interpretation had been advanced by John Keown of the University of Leicester in his book, *Abortion, Doctors and the Law*. Keown declared that abortion had been left by the common law courts to be resolved in the ecclesiastical or church courts. He argued that the fact that common law courts did not regularly punish abortion did not establish that such conduct was permissible at common law.[19]

The *Roe* Court's interpretation of the early common law scholars, Sir William Stanford and William Lambarde was also challenged in *Webster*. The argument conceded that:

Two Sixteenth Century authorities on common law criminal pleadings denied that abortion was a felony. 1 W. Stanford, *Pleas of the Crown* ch. 13 (1557); W. Lambarde, *Of the Office of the Justice of the Peace* 217–218 (1st ed. 1581). Yet an early formbook, which went through four editions between 1506 and 1544, included a form indictment for abortion by physical assault on the mother, *Boke of the Justyces of the Peas*, c. vi, fol. iii (1515).[20]

Alternative explanations were suggested to the Court to explain why Stanford and Lambarde had "denied that abortion was a felony." One theory was that these common law authorities were only "reflecting the inconclusiveness" of the reported decisions which existed at that time. A second theory was that by saying abortion was not a felony, Stanford and Lambarde really meant to say that "it was a crime less than a felony." The theory that Stanford and Lambarde believed that abortion could only be brought up in a church court was also disputed.

The *Roe* Court's interpretation of still other prominent common law scholars was also debated in *Webster* briefs. In *Roe*, the justices had concluded that Sir Edward Coke's definition of post-quickening abortion as a misdemeanor (a felony only if the fetus died after a live birth) was not the common law standard of the day. The Court in *Webster* was asked to reevaluate Coke and, in addition, a case of 1601 known as *R. v. Sims*, 75 Eng. Rep. 1075 (Q. B. 1601). The *Roe* Court had apparently dismissed this precedent as a "mooted" or argued, but not decided, issue. The new interpretation argued that *Sims* had become a precedent—whether an actual case decision or not—and that when coupled with a case known as *R. v. Webb* (1602) would prove that abortion was an offense at common law. Finally, the *Webster* Court was urged to reexamine the *Roe* Court's position on the views of Sir Matthew Hale. Hale had denied that an "abortion-induced death of a child born alive [was] a homicide" and the *Roe* Court had noted this position. Arguing that an earlier Hale treatise had followed Coke, pro-life scholars and lawyers urged the *Webster* Court to remember that Coke, not Hale, had long been considered the "Father of the Common Law" and to give more weight to his view.[21] Thus when the oral argument opened in *Webster*, the Court confronted divergent views of English common law scholars presented by the opposing sides in the case. And as Justice Antonin Scalia noted, each side cited ancient precedents and treatises that could be checked. Legal authorities on both sides of the Atlantic had compiled records, translated manuscripts and researched the historical context in which the great scholars of the English common law had functioned. From Bracton in the thirteenth century to Blackstone in the eighteenth century, significant data were available for analysis of the status of abortion in early English common law precedents.

EVALUATING ENGLISH COMMON LAW SCHOLARS: BRACTON TO BLACKSTONE

English legal scholars had not found the "common law" as a settled body of doctrine and rules in England. English common law was not a set of legislative rules adopted by Parliament. Instead, it developed over the centuries as "case" law or judicial decisions that set legal standards. English judges decided cases by adhering to precedents or reports of how similar issues had been decided by their counterparts in earlier times. This data could be obtained in several ways. It might appear in the written records of courts throughout the land. English courts such as Common Pleas and King's Bench preserved proceedings of the cases which were presented to them for argument and decision. Over time vast collections, or rolls, of court actions accumulated and these could be referred to by judges who sought to establish a predictable and uniform standard to deal with similar offenses at different time periods.[22] In addition to the written records of court cases and proceedings, treaties and books summarizing the judicial actions became available. Since these were shorter in length and were more easily attainable than the official court rolls, these books assumed great importance in conveying how various issues had been settled in earlier times. In general, the authors of the legal treatises included references to specific case decisions. The treatise would identify the presiding justices, the date of the decision, the case facts and questions. Then the decision or holding itself would be stated. Sometimes direct quotes from the original case rolls would be used.

All of the scholars and legal authorities involved in publishing such treatises included their own comments and appraisals. Their own analysis of issues and decisions thus assumed a significant place. Since it was difficult for ordinary justices throughout the country to have access to the actual court records, they came to rely on the more easily obtained treatises. Thus the writings of English common law authorities became the primary means for conveying precedents and establishing the principles of the English common law.[23]

These authorities, with their summarizing and analyzing of the developing precedents in England, had an impact beyond the confines of that country. American colonial leaders stocked their personal libraries with these volumes. Jefferson, Madison, and Adams, among others, read and mastered the works of the English common law commentators. In the pre-Revolutionary period, aspiring American lawyers often went to England and enrolled at the Inns of Court—English law schools—for legal study. One of the major objectives of these American students was the accumulation of a library that would provide material necessary for a successful legal practice in colonial America. Among the English common law scholars and authorities most widely read and studied both in England and America were Bracton, Stanford, Coke, Hale, Hawkins, and Blackstone. All of these authorities had, at some point, dealt with the issue of abortion.[24]

Henry de Bracton and Abortion

Henry de Bracton's multi-volume work entitled *De Legibus et Consuetudinibus Angliae* (On the Laws and Customs of England) was written in the thirteenth century: the first reference to abortion in English law appeared in this treatise. Bracton, a royal justice on the Court of King's Bench and judge of the assize (circuit) for the southwestern counties in England, had become dissatisfied with the lack of organization in the common law. He had personal access to numerous documents in which case decisions had been recorded by earlier judges and decided to organize these into a treatise available to all judges. To this end he collected some 2,000 case decisions handed down between 1216–1240. Bracton's treatise was designed to systematize legal thought by showing legal developments in England through the presentation of factual, decided cases. "The law," he said, "should go from precedent to precedent." He affirmed and perpetuated what became a permanent characteristic of English law, namely, dependence upon decided cases; his treatise became the leading textbook on the laws of England.[25]

Bracton wrote during a time period in which many different types of courts and law existed in England. Among these were the long-established church courts as well as the newly emerging royal courts. The church or ecclesiastical courts were, owing to their extensive jurisdiction, formidable rivals to the royal or secular courts. Bracton himself was a member of the clergy; he had been educated at the cathedral schools and studied the canon law. However, Bracton's appointment to various judicial posts in the royal courts gave him a primary loyalty to them.

Bracton thought that the jurisdiction of the church courts went too far
in a number of areas. He was not content to leave questions about wills
and issues of inheritance to the control of the church courts. However,
Bracton also recognized that the royal courts of his day had no rules to
deal with all of these matters.[26]

Bracton apparently believed that abortion should be within the control
and jurisdiction of the state or royal courts. This would have involved
moving abortion issues from the church courts' jurisdiction to that of
the Court of King's Bench. However, throughout Bracton's career that
shift of jurisdiction did not occur. As a result, he himself as a royal judge
did not decide any abortion issue. However, he did include in his treatise
a statement on abortion. Bracton's frame of reference for this pro-
nouncement—the only one he apparently made—was his clerical background. He had studied Aristotle and the Greek scholars on stages of
fetal development. He had also given a great amount of time to a study
of the canon law. His environment was one in which canon law, Roman
civil law, and English judicial practices were not yet clearly differentiated.
From this milieu therefore Bracton took his statement on abortion. It
was, in fact, a restatement of the church law that existed at that time
and read as follows:

If there be anyone who strikes a pregnant woman or gives her poison whereby
he causes an abortion, if the foetus be already formed or animated, and especially
if it be animated, he commits homicide.[27]

The statement stood alone in Bracton's treatise, unaccompanied by explanations or by case precedents to confirm it. In fact since it was the
canon law position, there was no need to elaborate. The meaning of
"formed or animated" according to the writing of Gratian, church law
scholar of the early 1100s, was clear. "Formed" referred to a fetus which
demonstrated the physical characteristics of a human being. "Animated"
referred to the point at which this physical form received a soul. Under
canon law according to Gratian, abortion was murder only when the
soul was present. Canon law authorities followed Aristotle in holding
that ensoulment occurred in forty days for a male and eighty days for
a female. Canon law also recognized two levels of homicide: voluntary
and accidental. Voluntary homicide was "true murder" and accidental
was "manslaughter" according to the treatises of Bernard of Pavia, an
authority Bracton studied.[28]

Bracton's statement on abortion used these terms which were so central
to the church or canon law concepts of his day. His emphasis on "animation" or "ensoulment" was part of the church's theory then. However,
his inclusion of this comment in his treatise in the absence of English
common law case precedent meant that later English secular courts could

consider it "dictum," personal opinion apart from the holding of a case decision. Recognizing it as the canon law position and observing that there was no record of actual litigation among Bracton's 2,000 case examples, some later English common law scholars defined the statement as Bracton's personal opinion. It was not actual practice in any recorded case at common law.

Bracton's statement was significant, however, because it led to the English common law doctrine known as "quickening." Bracton's use of the words "formed" and "animated" helped to set the stage for the question: "At what point—if any—does the abortion of a fetus become a crime?"

English Common Law Scholars and "Quickening": Pre-Viability Standards from the Thirteenth Century

As the common law began to develop systematically in the years following Bracton, the practical-minded judges of the English courts began to look away from ancient church authorities. Tangled disputes of medieval church fathers over whether or not an impregnated ovum possessed a soul seemed far removed from the day-to-day problems of inheritance and tort actions.[29] The English common law therefore began to develop its own system and way of thinking apart from church law. English judges, whenever possible, based their case decisions on what other English judges had already decided. Whenever case precedents and parliamentary statutes did not exist, the pragmatic approach to decision making became the rule. This approach was clearly demonstrated in the case of unborn children. Judges developed the doctrine of quickening which equated movement with life. Judges found the quickening distinction to be legally useful in capital punishment cases; in inheritance and property rights cases the quickening doctrine did not prove useful; and in questions of prenatal injuries judges and courts were divided. However, for procured abortion issues, quickening became the key in the common law's attitude toward abortion.

If some distinction had to be made in the stages of a woman's pregnancy, a clearly demonstrable one was the stage at which the fetus began to move. Anyone touching the mother could feel that the fetus was alive. This was a practical way to deal with cases of women who, as convicted felons, were under a death sentence. Under English common law if the woman was "quick with child" her execution would be postponed. Judges could summon a "jury of matrons" to examine the woman. If they could detect no movement the execution was carried out immediately. This approach was first recorded in English practice in 1349 in the so-called *Jury of Matron's Case*.[30] Later, common law authorities such as Blackstone summarized the law's holding by stating that women who were "barely with child" but not "quick" could not postpone the execution of their sentence. American judges also followed this distinction between quickened and non-quickened fetuses in the case of female criminals. In 1778 Massachusetts executed Mrs. Bathsheba Spooner for the murder of her husband. At the time Mrs. Spooner was pregnant but not "quick with child."[31]

Cases that raised issues of inheritance and property rights did not lend themselves well to use of the quickening distinction. Thus the common law in areas of devolution of property, trusts, and illegitimacy ignored quickening. In these cases the standard was that of "live birth." Courts operated under a "legal fiction" which preserved rights until a living child was born. If live birth failed to transpire, the rights preserved by the court's actions would be lost. In addition, cases raising problems of prenatal injuries (torts) and the right of recovery of damages used a live birth standard and quickening was not used in such cases.[32] In the United States the ruling precedent until after World War II was that a quick fetus suffering prenatal injuries from a negligent defendant could not recover damages apart from its mother.[33] Following World War II state statutes tried to reverse this holding by permitting recovery if the fetus was viable, or at least quick when the injuries were sustained. However, in such cases, a live birth was still generally necessary. Moreover, if the object of recovery for prenatal injuries was to compensate a living person (the baby) who bore the injuries caused by another's negligence, then whether the injury occurred when the fetus was "quick" or not seemed irrelevant. Thus quickening as a common law doctrine seemed to be uniquely associated only with procured abortion; some of the great common law scholars focused on it and others apparently ignored it.[34]

Sir William Stanford

The early common law scholars who came after Bracton operated in a legal system that was becoming more free from church court influences and which was developing its own doctrines and procedures. One of the earliest and most influential of the English common law scholars was Sir William Stanford. Born in 1509, Stanford had received a university education at Oxford. Unlike Bracton who had studied in church schools and learned law as a cleric and royal clerk, Stanford had received his legal education at Gray's Inn, one of the traditional Inns of Court or English law schools. He served as a member of Parliament, as a teacher of law, as a crown prosecutor, and as a justice. Stanford's systematic treatise on English law, *Les Plees del Coron* (The Pleas of the Crown), was published in 1557 and made extensive use of specific case precedent. He summarized the common law as it had developed up to that time, and presented cases and running commentary. In some areas he challenged Bracton's views by citing specific case examples to demonstrate a difference between judicial holdings and Bracton's comments. This was particularly true in the area of abortion.[35]

Stanford's analysis of abortion was quite different from Bracton's. Whereas Bracton's comment had linked abortion and homicide, Stanford's treatise stated, "If a man kill a child in the womb of its mother: this is not a felony, neither shall he forfeit anything."[36] Unlike Bracton's commentary, however, Stanford found precedents in two famous fourteenth-century cases now sometimes known as the *Twinslayer's Case*, (1347) and the *Abortionist's Case*, (1348). These cases had been decided after Bracton's time and Stanford stated that their holdings had contradicted Bracton's dictum.

The *Twinslayer's Case*, 1 Edw.3(1327) was a case involving a woman in an advanced stage of pregnancy and carrying twins. She had been beaten severely and directly afterwards had given birth. One twin was stillborn, but the other was alive. This twin was named John and baptized according to the custom of the day. However, two days later he died. The man who had beaten the mother was indicted. He pled "not guilty" and the charges were dismissed. According to the judges no felony had been committed.

The second case which Stanford cited concerning abortion had occurred in 1348. Now known simply as the *Abortionist's Case* was summarized in the court records in the following words:

One was indicted for killing a child in the womb of its mother, and the opinion was that he shall not be arrested on the indictment since no baptismal name was in the indictment, and also it is difficult to know whether he killed the child or not.[37]

Stanford's presentation and analysis of these abortion cases raise significant issues. One of these is the importance of a baptismal name. In that era an infant was baptized and given a Christian name which was clearly entered in the register of the local parish church in which the baptismal ceremony took place. Since the state made no effort to record births, this church record served as the only official documentation of an individual's birthdate, proper name, and parentage. It was the only proof of his or her legal existence. Without a registered baptismal name one lacked legal personhood.[38] The judges in the *Abortionist's Case* apparently viewed an indictment for the killing of an unborn, unnamed child as improper in its form and as one reason for dismissal of charges. At other times, however, judges focused more on the issue of proof that an accused had caused the death of an infant in its mother's womb.

Stanford's cases and analyses do not seem to be dealing with cases of procured or desired abortion. However, they are essential and critical precedents in this area because they appeared to accept the principle that the fetus had no legal existence until after live birth. Stanford's commentary on the two case precedents demonstrated that for a charge of murder to be brought, the person killed had to be *in rerum natura*. This meant that something existed independently in the world of secular reality as, for example, a live born baby. It is Stanford, therefore, who became the primary English common law authority for the theory that, at common law, abortion even after quickening was not an offense of any kind. The case precedents which he cited appeared to run counter to Bracton's statement on abortion, and in fact Stanford insisted that Bracton's view had not prevailed in English courts and had been con-tradicted by actual practice. He considered Bracton's statement to be dictum only, not a holding in any case, and a false statement of what the common law really held. Stanford's summary indicated that he in-terpreted the existing decisions to say that abortion was not only not a felony, it was not a crime at all.[39]

Stanford and Levels or Types of Crimes: Felony and Misdemeanor

Stanford indicated that a person who caused the death of a child in the womb of its mother was not to forfeit anything. In cases of lesser crimes below the level of felonies—sometimes called "misprisions" or misdemeanors—an individual might be required to pay a fine or forfeit goods or possessions. "Misprision" was a term commonly used to refer to concealment of knowledge of a crime without having participated in it. Over time the term "misprision" was used to characterize offenses below the degree of felony. It was a term used only at secular law and dealt with only by non-ecclesiastical courts. The penalty for an offense characterized as a "misprision" was usually a "forefeiture of chattels or goods" or perhaps "fines and imprisonment."[40] In modern terminology "misdemeanor" refers to offenses below the degree of felony and often involves payment of fines. Stanford's commentary had noted that in the case of misdemeanors, forfeiture of goods was an appropriate penalty. However, no one could be required to pay fines or forfeit goods for "kill[ing] a child in the womb of its mother." This was no crime of felony and not even a misdemeanor.

William Lambarde and Michael Dalton

Following Stanford among the English common law authorities were two scholars who, although important, served mainly to restate and re-affirm Stanford's work. The first of these was William Lambarde who wrote his treatise in 1581, and the second was Michael Dalton, writing in 1618. William Lambarde, like Stanford, studied at the Inns of Court at Lincoln's Inn. He was famous as an early legal historian who compiled and translated Anglo-Saxon laws. Appointed a justice of the peace in 1579, by 1592 he was a justice in chancery and keeper of the Court Rolls. In 1601 Queen Elizabeth I made him keeper of the Tower records. Lambarde's major treatise dealing with the developing English common law was entitled *Eirenarcha: or of the Office of the Justices of Peace.* Printed in 1581 in two volumes, it was praised for its clear and unaffected style. It remained the standard authority for many years; even Sir William Blackstone later recommended its study. Lambarde's use of numerous case references and examples of crimes and penalties helped local judges to decide current problems in the common law tradition. His statements on abortion became influential because of the widespread use of his treatise.[41]

Lambarde defined abortion as the destruction of the fetus while within the body of the woman. He repeated the two precedents used by Stanford, the *Twinslayer's Case* (1327) and the *Abortionist's Case* (1348), and then gave his own summary of the common law. It read as follows:

If the child be destroied in the mother's belly, the destroier is no manslayer, nor Felone. The child is not reckoned to be *In rerum natura*, until it bee born, though M. Bracton taketh it to be Homicide....(after the foetus shall have been ensouled.)[42]

Lambarde set aside Bracton, as had Stanford, and both authorities focused on live birth and separation from the mother as the essential factor. One could be charged and tried for infanticide but not for abortion. Quickening was not significant.

Michael Dalton was an English common law scholar of the seventeenth century. Dalton's major treatise, published in 1618, was entitled *The Countrey Justice.* Dalton followed the tradition of Lambarde in explaining the common law through extensive citation of cases decided principally by the justices of the peace.[43] When dealing with the issue of abortion, Dalton confirmed the precedents and the summaries of Lambarde and Stanford. His own statement read thus:

If a man kill an infant in his mother's wombe, by our law, this is no felony: neither shall he forfeit anything for such offense: and whether the child die within her body, or shortly after her deliverie, it maketh no difference.[44]

For Dalton the difficulty of proving that an action had caused the death of an unborn fetus was one which made a charge of murder or homicide inappropriate. A child "not born" was not *in rerum natura,* and therefore not the subject of murder. Killing such a child was not murder or manslaughter. Dalton did not comment on a situation in which a child, born alive and showing on its body the injuries received while in the mother's womb, subsequently died. A case of this nature had arisen in 1601. Known as *Sim's Case*[45] it had been argued and discussed by the justices of the period but apparently not authoritatively decided. There was a dispute as to whether this was a case of assault and battery against the mother or appropriate for a charge of homicide. Since it had not been resolved, Dalton apparently thought that no precedent existed at common law and it had no impact on his writings.

Sir Edward Coke

The writings of Sir Edward Coke whose career peaked during the early seventeenth century exercised a vast influence on the development of the common law in England and wherever Englishmen planted colonies around the world. He is best remembered for his role in defending the rights of the English Parliament and the law courts against the political ambitions of the early Stuart kings, James I and Charles I. In addition, Coke also greatly influenced abortion law.

The son of a well-to-do country gentleman and lawyer, Coke attended Cambridge University and studied to become a barrister at the Inns of Court in London. He quickly earned a reputation for his legal skills, especially his encyclopedic knowledge of case precedents and the intricacies of the judicial process. He held some of the most important legal and political offices in England: recorder of London; solicitor-general; Speaker of the House of Commons; attorney general from 1594–1606; Chief Justice of Common Pleas, 1606–1612; and Chief Justice of King's Bench, 1612–1616. He was also knighted and made a privy councillor, enjoying royal favor until his judicial opposition to James I's claims for the royal powers brought about his dismissal in 1616. He authored the famous Petition of Right in 1628 which asserted the principle that the king was under the law, not above it.[46]

Coke was respected by friend and foe for his fierce and stubborn advocacy of the principles in which he believed, and as attorney general he successfully prosecuted many cases. An able and even unscrupulous advocate for any case or cause he favored, Coke was frequently involved in litigation himself. He managed to defend himself successfully in the church courts for marrying irregularly and without a license. On another occasion he persuaded the Court of Star Chamber to drop charges against him for his actions in forcing his own daughter into a political marriage against her will. As a judge, Coke asserted the independence of the judiciary and the supremacy of the common law courts with lasting effect.[47]

Coke admired, indeed almost worshipped, the medieval English common law on which he wrote extensively. He is especially known for his famous *Reports* and his *Institutes*. The former is a collection of cases intended to educate students of law through the record of arguments and judgments made and given in cases. The *Institutes* are a four-volume commentary on English law. The encyclopedic nature of these commentaries and the clarity and directness of Coke's style made the treatise both popular and influential, and they were quoted in courts both in England and America. It was in the third volume of the *Institutes* that Coke set forth his position on abortion, which read as follows:

If a woman be quick with childe, and by a potion or otherwise killeth it in her womb; or if a man beat her, whereby the childe dieth in her body, and she is delivered of a dead childe, this is a great misprision, and no murder; but if the childe be born alive, and dieth of the potion, battery, or other cause, this is murder: for in law it is accounted a reasonable creature, *in rerum natura*, when it is born alive. And the Book in 1E.3 [the *Twinslayer's Case*, 1327] was never holden for law. And 3 Ass. p. 2 is but a repetition of that case. (See Stan. [Stanford] P. Cor. 21C.; see 22E.3. Cor. 263 [the *Abortionist's Case*, 1348]) and so horrible an offense should not go unpunished. And so was the law holden in Bracton's time. . . . And here with agreeth Fleta: and herein the law is grounded upon the law of God, which saith, "whoso sheddeth man's blood, by man shall his blood be shed: for in the image of God made he man" [Genesis 9:6]. If a man counsell a woman to kill the child within her wombe, when it shall be born, and after she is delivered of the child, she killeth it: the counsellor is an accessory to the murder, and yet at the time of the commandment, or counsell, no murder could be committed of the child *in utero matris*, the reason of which case proveth well the other case.[48]

This quote and other historical data demonstrate that Coke considered abortion after quickening a "horrible" offense which should be punished. He apparently based part of his view here on Bracton's statements about "animation" which Coke interpreted as "quickening."

Coke set aside the so-called *Twinslayer's Case* and the *Abortionist's Case* which were the two major common law case precedents on abortion at that time. Their holdings were contrary to Coke's own opinion, and he stated that these cases were "never holden for law." Coke wanted to bring abortion under the control of his own court and to take it away from the church courts. As a judge Coke had engaged in a long and bitter series of major conflicts with the church courts and believed that they were unable to deter abortion.

Apparently the courts had not heard any abortion cases since the sixteenth century. The last two cases on record had occurred during the reigns of Henry VII and Henry VIII. With no contemporary, successful prosecutions for abortion in the church courts, and no common law case precedents that agreed with his personal views, Coke nevertheless developed an analogy to infanticide in order to pronounce abortion after quickening a "great misprision."

It was Coke's introduction of the classification of "misprision" or misdemeanor to characterize one type of post-quickened abortion that would be his most notable contribution to this policy area. Coke's classifications of abortion were stated in his treatise. He did not deal with abortion before quickening, thus apparently leaving its status as "no crime" intact. After quickening, an abortion which led to a still birth was a "great misprision": it was "no murder" and hence no felony even though the fetus had been quick. But it was a misdemeanor which could be punished by secular courts with at least a fine. Post-quickened abortion followed by a live birth and then subsequent death was, however, murder if the child's death could be linked to the "potion" or "battery."

Although Coke's *Third Institute*'s section on crimes of "misprision" did not mention abortion, his other pronouncements on abortion were read in the American colonies and followed in some court proceedings. His views on different levels of punishment for post-quickened abortion— although not apparently founded on the legal practices and cases of his day—influenced American courts and legislators well into the twentieth century.[49]

Sir Matthew Hale, William Hawkins, and Sir William Blackstone

Three major commentators and legal scholars in the years following Coke also had significant impact on the dissemination of the case principles which constituted the English common law on abortion. These authorities were: Sir Matthew Hale (1609–1676), William Hawkins (1673–1746), and Sir William Blackstone (1723–1780). Each man produced numerous treatises, articles, and summaries which were eagerly sought and used by contemporary judges and legislators in both England and America. Hale's *The History of the Pleas of the Crown* was well known in America. Hawkins' great work was his *Treatise of the Pleas of the Crown*, which was printed first in 1716 and then went through four additional printings. Blackstone's multi-volume *Commentaries* (1765–69) were standard in early American legal library collections of lawyers and scholars.

Sir Matthew Hale was born into a lawyer's family: his father was a barrister of Lincoln's Inn. Hale followed in his footsteps and entered Lincoln's Inn as a student in 1628. During the English Civil War his sympathies lay with the Royalists and he served as counsel for prominent peers. Once the Commonwealth under Cromwell was established, however, he swore allegiance to it. This was essential for lawyers in 1649. By 1654 Hale's reputation was growing and he was created a justice of the Court of Common Pleas. He retained this position until Cromwell's death. Having taken an active part in the restoration of Charles II, he was rewarded with the office of lord chief baron of the exchequer. In

1671 he was created Chief Justice of the Court of King's Bench until ill health forced his retirement. Hale was regarded as a superior lawyer. His contemporaries praised his "immense industry, knowledge, and sagacity." His arguments were described as solid and clear in tone and content. It is stated that "he was allowed on all hands to be the most profound lawyer of his time." His authority came at last to be regarded as all but infallible.[50]

Hale wrote a number of learned treatises on English law; his judicial opinions also were well known. In his major legal treatise he presented his understanding of the status of abortion at common law, his summaries of the case precedents dealing with abortion, and his own analysis of Sir Edward Coke's views. Hale rehearsed the two major case precedents originally cited by Sir William Stanford, and summarized the so-called *Twinslayer's Case*, (1327) and the *Abortionist's Case*, (1348) thus:

> If a woman be quick or great with child, if she take, or another give her any potion to make an abortion, or if a man strike her, whereby the child within her is killed, it is not murder nor manslaughter by the law of England, because it is not yet *in rerum natura*, tho it be a great crime, and by the law of Moses [Exodus 21:22] was punishable with death, nor can it legally be known whether it were kild or not, 22E.3.P. Coron. 263 [the *Abortionist's Case* (1348)]. If after such child were born alive, and baptized, and after die of the stroke given to the mother, this is not homicide, 1E3 23.P. Coron. 146 [the *Twinslayer's Case* (1327)].[51]

For Hale, the common law as decided in the two ancient case precedents did not regard abortion as either murder or manslaughter. There was no "quickening" distinction. Hale's reference to religious dogma concerning abortion apparently was intended to point out that abortion had always been dealt with by the ecclesiastical or church courts only. Abortion was clearly a crime under canon or church law and Hale asserted this in his summary.

Hale's summary also raised the question of the self-induced abortion. In describing the sources of abortion Hale had mentioned three possibilities: first, the woman herself might take something: second, someone else might give the pregnant woman a "potion" to cause an abortion; third, a "man" might "strike" a pregnant woman, thus causing an abortion. Case precedents decided by the English common law courts in the few cases decided after 1327 had not clearly dealt with the first of these possibilities, self-induced abortion. Judicial opinions had concentrated on individuals other than the pregnant woman. In general these were not persons the pregnant woman had procured to affect her condition.

Hale, however, did hear and decide one case in which this latter situation occurred. A charge of murder was brought against an abortioner who caused the death of a pregnant woman. Although the case lacked a name, Hale described it in his treatise and set forth the facts and his decision. He stated that a "potion" had been given a woman who was with child and that it had killed her. The case came before him at a court session in 1670 in the town of Bury St. Edmunds. Hale declared that the abortioner who had administered the potion was guilty of the murder of the woman. He did not mention the fetus. Hale did not cite any case precedent to uphold his decision, so apparently he regarded it as innovative and without precedent in a common law court. It would prove to be an important precedent in future cases, particularly in America.[52]

A second major commentator and legal scholar who made an impact on abortion law in the years following Coke was William Hawkins. Born in 1673, he graduated from Cambridge and studied law at the Inner Temple. He became a barrister and then a justice and became famous primarily for his scholarly book entitled *Treatise of the Pleas of the Crown*. The first edition appeared in 1716 and four additional editions followed, including a condensed version that circulated widely. Hawkins also wrote an abridgment of Coke's *Institutes* and thus became an authority on Coke's works. [53] Hawkins did not incorporate Hale's writings on abortion; he used Coke's statements instead. Hawkins's statement on abortion paraphrased Coke in these words:

And it was anciently [by Bracton] holden, that the causing of an abortion by giving a potion to, or striking, a woman big with child, was murder: But at this Day, it is said to be a great misprision [by Coke] only, and no murder.[54]

Hawkins himself did not decide any abortion cases; he did not analyze Coke or question his statements either. His aim was primarily to summarize existing authorities although he did not use all of them.

Sir William Blackstone, the last of the great English common law authorities to exercise significant influence in America, began his legal career at the Middle Temple where he became a law student in 1741. He had received his undergraduate education at Oxford where he had shown interest in literature and classical studies. Blackstone was not a gifted orator and did not do well in his court presentations as a legal counsel. As a result he turned his attention to the organization of legal materials and became successful as a legal scholar. Oxford employed him as the first teacher of common law at the university. Before this time legal subjects were not taught in the undergraduate curriculum at Oxford or Cambridge. Blackstone, however, was given an endowed chair which enabled him to deliver lectures on the history and development of law. His success as a teacher won him a judge's robe, but his major fame came as a result of his publication in legal history. Blackstone had decided to prepare his lectures for publication in the form of a general survey of English law. He produced the first volume of his *Commentaries* in 1765 and the other three volumes at intervals during the next four years. Few books have been more successful than the *Commentaries*, which went through eight editions during Blackstone's lifetime alone. Laymen turned to him because he made English law readable, and it is still to Blackstone that English law students turn for a general view of the subject. His name is heard in both English and American courts, and judges fortify their decisions by quoting his statements of the law. It was said that by 1775 Americans had bought as many copies of Blackstone's *Commentaries* as had been sold in England.[55]

Blackstone's statements on abortion occurred in volumes one and four of his *Commentaries*. He concentrated on summarizing Bracton and Coke and in the process clearly addressed the doctrine of quickening. Volume one, published in 1765, contained the following statement:

Life . . . begins in contemplation of the law as soon as an infant is able to stir in a mother's womb. For if a woman is quick with child, and by a potion, or otherwise, killeth it in her womb; or if anyone beat her, where by the child dieth in her body and she is delivered of a dead child; this, though not murder, was by the ancient law homicide or manslaughter (see Bracton). But at present it is not looked upon in quite so atrocious a light, though it remains a very heinous misdemeanor (see Coke).[56]

And in Volume four, published in 1769, Blackstone repeated the same thought in another passage, "To kill a child in its mother's womb is now no murder, but a great misprision."[57]

AMERICAN JUDGES AND ENGLISH AUTHORITIES

American legal thought basically followed the English common law doctrines on abortion as described in the treatises of these English legal scholars. Some American courts focused on the opinions of Coke and Blackstone; others paid greater attention to Stanford and Hale. All dealt with the English common law doctrine of quickening. Analysis of U.S. court decisions demonstrates the extent to which English legal authorities affected American abortion policy. The most significant early U.S. court case dealing with abortion was decided in Massachusetts in 1812. It was known as *Commonwealth v. Bangs*, 9 Mass. 387 (1812). An abortionist named Isaiah Bangs, indicted for performing an abortion, was acquitted because it had not been established that the woman was quick with child. The *Bangs* case became the ruling judicial precedent in cases of abortion in the United States through the first half of the nineteenth century and in many states for some years later. Its holding and dictum demonstrated a number of facts about abortion policy in America up to this time. First, prosecutions for abortion prior to quickening were virtually unheard of in U.S. courts at this time. Second, pre-quickening abortion was not regarded as a crime and was beyond the scope of the law as far as courts were concerned. Third, American courts with their English common law traditions and doctrines exhibited a tolerant attitude toward abortion. Most American courts understood the common law to say that abortion of an unquickened fetus was not a criminal act. In this interpretation they were clearly influenced by the treatises of English common law scholars like Stanford and Hale as well as Coke and Blackstone. Fourth, some U.S. courts in the period following *Bangs* clearly held that abortion of a quick fetus was a misdemeanor if it was charged and proved beyond a reasonable doubt that the fetus was indeed quick. In this interpretation the influence of Coke and Blackstone alone was most pronounced. The lack of court cases of pre-quickened abortion and the refusal of most prosecutors to try to bring indictments for post-quickened abortion due to difficulty of proof, meant that abortion convictions in courts of law were rare.

These conclusions about the effect which English common law had on American legal thought can be demonstrated by an examination of court cases that did arise during the nineteenth century. Even the enactment of state statutes dealing with abortion did not deter the courts from their traditional reliance on the ancient doctrine of English common law, particularly that of quickening. One case of particular significance was *Commonwealth v. Parker*, 50 Mass. 263 (1845). Chief Justice Lemuel Shaw of the Massachusetts Supreme Court refused in an 1845 case to convict an abortionist, Luceba Parker, because quickening had not been proved in any of the indictments lodged against her. Her actions, therefore, according to Chief Justice Shaw were not punishable at common law. The *Parker* case also contained dicta that used Sir Matthew Hale's 1670 decision at Bury St. Edmunds. Hale ruled that an abortioner whose actions caused the death of the mother could be held to have committed murder. Chief Justice Shaw repeated Hale's decision in the following dictum in *Parker*:

The use of violence upon a woman, with an intent to procure her miscarriage, without her consent, . . . would be indictable at common law. So where, upon a similar attempt by drugs or instruments, the death of the mother ensues, the party making such an attempt, with or without the consent of the woman, is guilty of murder of the mother.

Shaw, like Hale, made no mention of the fetus.

The 1850s brought forth a number of cases. They came from as far south as Alabama; as far west as the Iowa frontier; and as far north as Maine. In all of these diverse areas of the country local courts and justices continued to look to English scholars for guidance in abortion decisions. A Pennsylvania court in *Mills v. Commonwealth*, 13 Pa. 631 (1850) decided that Coke's statements about abortion justified the state of Pennsylvania in not demanding that quickening be proved. Focusing on Coke's *Third Institute*, the state supreme court admitted that Massachusetts and other states had reached a different conclusion based on the same authority. However, the Pennsylvania court insisted that the "well settled and established doctrines of the common law," which Coke had emphasized, primarily stressed the "flagrant crim[inality] . . . of abortion." They believed that Coke's intent was more important than his actual words and provided sufficient excuse for the state to reach all acts of abortion.

In Maine, however, an 1851 case followed the interpretations given the common law by the justices in Massachusetts rather than those in Pennsylvania. In the case of *Smith v. State*, 33 Me. 48(1851), the Maine state supreme court required that a prosecution for abortion prove that quickening had occurred. Said the court,

At common law it was no offense to perform an operation upon a pregnant woman by her consent, for the purpose of procuring an abortion . . . unless the woman was "quick with child." . . . If, before the mother had become sensible of its motion in the womb, it was not a crime; if afterwards, when it was considered by the common law, that the child had a separate and independent existence, it was held highly criminal.

The Maine state supreme court thus asserted the traditional views of Stanford and Hale and incorporated Coke's view that abortion after quickening was a "great misprision." The Maine court also used this case to assert Sir Matthew Hale's Bury St. Edmunds decision of 1670. The court made it clear that in its understanding of the common law, a woman's abortionist faced a risk. The words of the Maine court, repeating Hale, stated that, "If medicine is given to a female to procure an abortion, which kills her, the party administering will be guilty of her murder."

By the 1870s a number of state legislatures had adopted laws dealing with abortion and their state courts were called upon to interpret and apply these statutes. State courts in New York imposed quickening guidelines when interpreting and applying that state's early abortion statutes of 1829 and 1869, as in the case of *Evans v. People*, 49 N.Y. 86 (1872). In the initial trial the jury demanded evidence to show at what point in time the fetus had quickened. The trial judge, however, instructed the jury to ignore this criteria since the state statute had dropped the word "quickened" from its provision. Nevertheless, on appeal, the court of appeals resurrected the doctrine and applied it in a traditional, legal argument. Manslaughter was not the correct charge in this case, said the

court because under common law a miscarriage had never been punishable as manslaughter. A six-month premature delivery was considered
a miscarriage, and Evans therefore could not be charged with manslaughter under traditional English common law descriptions. In the
words of the judges,

It was error to charge that the death of a child could be caused or produced
before it had given evidence of life, had become "quick" in the womb, and that
the crime of manslaughter under the statute could be predicated on the destruction of the foetus before that period.

Thus the common law doctrine of quickening and the common law
definitions of crimes of manslaughter combined to influence the enforcement of the New York state statute. Jurors and judges alike continued to ask the traditional questions and to use known standards. The
influence of the English common law scholar, Sir Edward Coke, also
manifested itself in the *Evans* case. The court clearly distinguished between abortion before and after quickening and stated that

at common law an unsuccessful attempt to effect the destruction of an infant
"quick" in its mother's womb, appears to have been treated as a misdemeanor,
and an actual destruction of such infant as a high crime.

Before quickening, the *Evans* court continued, "although there may be
embryo life in the fetus, there is no living child." For the New York
court of appeals in 1872 these were such traditional, settled doctrines
of common law that they could not be ignored when courts interpreted
the state legislative statute.

Vague state statutes were thus brought into harmony with perceived
common law doctrine by state courts as they decided the cases that came
before them. Whenever statutes did not exist courts naturally had even
greater latitude. Although by the 1870s a number of court decisions had
been rendered by state courts throughout the United States, no court
could be required to follow its neighbor's footsteps. Courts were free
when state statutes were nonexistent or unclear to utilize American or
English precedents and to interpret the views of English common law
scholars.

During the 1880s and 1890s U.S. courts continued to talk about their
common law heritage and to identify and debate what they understood
to be the doctrines associated with abortion under the common law. The
North Carolina state supreme court in 1880 is a good example. In deciding the case of *State v. Slagle*, 83 N.C. 544 (1880) the state judges
reexamined the identical English precedent which Chief Justice Shaw
from Massachusetts had analyzed in the 1848 *Parker* case. They also

looked at the English statutory law. Finally they evaluated the various U.S. state court decisions and dismissed all but that of the state of Pennsylvania. Adopting the 1850 decision of *Mills v. Commonwealth*, the North Carolina judges defined it as being less restrictive of the common law's aims. Abortion, they held, was criminal not just after quickening, but at any stage. Both decisions seemed to be closer to the views of Bracton than to those of Coke, yet both seemed to echo Coke's justification that some agency must operate to punish "so horrible an offense." In choosing to abandon the quickening distinction the North Carolina court sought justification from its common law author. Courts thus seemed to take great pride in insisting upon their own interpretation of English legal authorities.

In the twentieth century state legislatures have often tried to draft statutes so that judges would not need to look beyond the words of the written law. Still, historic common law concepts have continued to appear, and courts have handed down decisions using the common law doctrine of quickening and citing the views of English legal scholars. Quickening clearly served in Georgia to differentiate between charges, for in the case of *Passley v. State*, 215 E. 230 (1942) a Georgia court stated that abortion of a non-quick fetus was not murder but only a misdemeanor. South Carolina courts made the same point in *State v. Steadman*, 214 S.C. 1 (1948) where the justices stated that,

Distinctions between the condition of the child before and after quickening have been recognized by providing a much more severe punishment for the destruction of a child after it has quickened than for the destruction of a child before it has quickened: distinctions in the light of the common law rule, and much earlier statutes in England."

Judges in Virginia also demonstrated their knowledge of common law and their determination to keep its ideas alive. In *Miller v. Bennett*, 190 VA. 162 (1940) the court reminded parties to the case that, "It was not an indictable offense at common law to procure an abortion before the woman had become quick with child." The New Jersey state supreme court during this same period declared that the common law had not traditionally held a woman to have committed an act of criminal abortion unless she were quick with child. Moreover, in the absence of clear legislative provisions concerning the woman, this preexisting common law would apply in New Jersey in assessing her acts. Such was the holding of the court in *In Re Vince*, 2 N.J. 443 (1949). And in a later case the New Jersey court again reminded the parties that "at common law induced abortion was a crime only after quickening."

Courts in Idaho, Nebraska, and Ohio among others also continued to refer to the common law doctrine of quickening. Usually this was done in judicial dictum and served to emphasize the difference between the new American legislative statutes and the old common law doctrines. One Ohio state court demonstrated this by noting in *State v. Tippie*, 89 Ohio St. 35 (1913), "The [state] statute does not require, as formerly and at common law, that the drug shall have been administered to a woman ... pregnant with a quick child." State courts also continued their established and traditional practice of evaluating the early English legal scholars' views on abortion and interpreting them in light of the current American problems.[58]

The U.S. Supreme Court in 1973 in *Roe v. Wade* cited many of these American state cases in which earlier courts had struggled to identify correctly the status of abortion in the treatises of the English common law scholars. The *Roe* Court observed: "[M]ost American courts ruled, in holding or dictum, that abortion of an *unquickened* fetus was not criminal under their received common law." This approach, according to the Court's documentation, followed the views of Stanford and Hale among others. However, the Court also pointed out that some U.S. courts had followed Coke and had declared that abortion of a *quick* fetus was a misdemeanor. Which of the state case precedents was correct? Ultimately, the *Roe* Court decided to follow those state court rulings that were based on Stanford and Hale. Their reason was that the courts who relied on Coke had done so "uncritical[ly]": they had not analyzed and questioned Coke's precedents as they should have.[59]

Yet the questions about the abortion position of these early English legal authorities still remained in the years following *Roe*. These questions emerged again to be debated in oral argument and briefs in 1989 in *Webster v. Reproductive Health Services*. Judges and scholars continued to search for definitive answers as each side in the abortion controversy sought to capture one of more of the English common law's great legal authorities for its position. American legal thought turned to its English roots as modern American jurists searched for fundamental liberties deeply rooted in this nation's traditions[60] to identify the scope and limits of abortion rights.

NOTES

1. Bob Woodward and Scott Armstrong, *The Brethren: Inside the Supreme Court* (New York: Simon and Schuster, 1979), pp. 183, 236. See also David M. O'Brien, *Storm Center*, 2d ed. (New York: Norton, 1990), pp. 23–59.
2. "Transcripts of Arguments Before High Court on Abortion Case," *New York Times*, April 27, 1989, pp. B12–B14.
3. Ibid.
4. Ibid.
5. Ibid.
6. Ibid., emphasis added.

7. Roe v. Wade, 410 U.S. 117 (1973).

8. Ibid.

9. Ibid.

10. Philip B. Kurland and Gerhard Casper, eds., *Landmark Briefs and Argument of the Supreme Court of the United States: Constitutional Law*, vol. 75 (Arlington, VA: University Publications of America, 1975), pp. 788–790. Hereafter cited as *Landmark Briefs and Argument*.

11. Ibid., pp. 114–15.

12. Ibid., p. 188.

13. Ibid., pp. 782–91.

14. Ibid., p. 526. Coke's sentence actually read *"no* murder." Edward Coke, *The Third Part of the Institutes of the Laws of England* (London: E & R Brooke, 1797), p. 50.

15. Ibid., pp. 526–27.

16. Ibid., pp. 818–29.

17. Roe v. Wade, 410 U.S. 117, 134 (1973).

18. Amicus Curiae Brief for the Committee for Public Justice, Webster v. Reproductive Health Services, 492 U.S. 490 (1989).

19. Ibid. See also John Keown, *Abortion, Doctors and the Law* (New York: Cambridge University Press, 1988), pp. 1–13.

20. Ibid.

21. Ibid.

22. W. S. Holdsworth, *A History of English Law*, 13 vols. (Boston: Little, Brown, 1937), vol. 2, pp. 232–59.

23. W. S. Holdsworth, *The Historians of Anglo-American Law* (Hamden, CT.: Archon Books, 1966), pp. 3–156.

24. Ibid.

25. Sir Leslie Stephen and Sir Sidney Lee, eds., *The Dictionary of National Biography*, vol. 2 (London: Oxford University Press, 1921), pp. 1,052–54.

26. Holdsworth, *A History of English Law*, vol. 2, p. 259.

27. Henry de Bracton, *De Legibus et Consuetudinibus Angliae (On the Laws and Customs of England)*, edited by George E. Woodbine, translated by Samuel E. Thorne, 4 vols. (Cambridge, MA: Belknap Press of Harvard, 1968–1977) vol. 2, p. 341.

28. John T. Noonan, Jr., "An Almost Absolute Value in History," in John T. Noonan, Jr., ed., *The Morality of Abortion: Legal and Historical Perspectives* (Cambridge, MA: Harvard University Press, 1970), pp. 3–59.

29. Roger J. Huser, *The Crime of Abortion in Canon Law* (Washington, DC: The Catholic University of America Press, 1942), pp. 41–42.

30. Jury of Matrons' Case, (1349), 82 Selden Society, Select Cases in the Court of King's Bench under Edward III, vol. 6.

31. Commonwealth v. Bathsheba Spooner, 2 Am. Crim. Trials I (1844). Case was decided in 1778.

32. Cyril C. Means, Jr., "The Law of New York Concerning Abortion and the Status of the Foetus," 14 *New York Law Forum* (1968), p. 418. See also In Re Well's Will, 221 N.Y.S. 714 (1927).

33. Dietrich v. Inhabitants of Northampton, 138 Mass. 14 (1884).

34. Jay L. Garfield and Patricia Hennessey, eds., *Abortion: Moral and Legal*

Perspectives (Amherst: The University of Massachusetts Press, 1984), pp. 62–64 and 276–88.

35. Stephen and Lee, eds., *The Dictionary of National Biography*, vol. 18, p. 887.

36. Quoted in Cyril C. Means, Jr., "The Phoenix of Abortional Freedom: Is a Penumbral or Ninth-Amendment Right About to Arise from the Nineteenth-Century Legislative Ashes of a Fourteenth Century Common Law Liberty?" 17 *New York Law Forum* (1971), p. 385.

37. Ibid., pp. 337–42.

38. Until modern times the baptismal name, also known as the Christian or simply the first name, was the only proper legal name a person had. The last name or surname came into use as a convenience, usually indicating a person's place of residence or occupation.

39. Means, Jr., "The Phoenix of Abortional Freedom." p. 341.

40. Holdsworth, *A History of English Law*, vol. 3, p. 341.

41. Stephen and Lee, eds., *Dictionary of National Biography*, vol. 11, pp. 438–39.

42. Means, Jr., "The Phoenix of Abortional Freedom," pp. 342–43.

43. Stephen and Lee, eds., *Dictionary of National Biography*, vol. 5, pp. 435–36.

44. Michael Dalton, *The Countrey Justice: Containing the Practice of the Justices of the Peace out of their Sessions* (New York: Arno Press Reprint, 1972), p. 221.

45. Sims Case, 75 Eng. Rep. 1075 (1601).

46. Holdsworth, *A History of English Law*, vol. 5, pp. 423, 437–80.

47. Stephen and Lee, eds., *The Dictionary of National Biography*, vol. 4, pp. 685–700. See also Catherine Bowen, *The Lion and the Throne: The Life and Times of Sir Edward Coke* (Boston: Little, Brown, 1956) pp. 342–70.

48. Coke, *Third Part of the Institutes*, pp. 50–51.

49. Means, Jr., "The Phoenix of Abortional Freedom." pp. 345–48.

50. Stephen and Lee, eds., *The Dictionary of National Biography*, vol. 8, pp. 901–9.

51. Matthew Hale, *History of the Pleas of the Crown*, vol. 1, (1736), p. 433.

52. Means, Jr., "The Phoenix of Abortional Freedom," pp. 349–50, 371–72.

53. Stephen and Lee, eds., *The Dictionary of National Biography*, vol. 9, pp. 230–31.

54. William Hawkins, *Treatise of the Pleas of the Crown*, vol. 1 (1716), p. 80.

55. Stephens and Lee, eds., *The Dictionary of National Biography*, vol. 2, pp. 595–602.

56. William Blackstone, *Commentaries on the Laws of England*, 4 vols., 1765–1769 (Birmingham, AL: Gryphon Legal Classics Library Edition, 1983), vol. 1, pp. 125–30.

57. Ibid., vol. 4, p. 198.

58. James C. Mohr, *Abortion in America: The Origin and Evolution of National Policy, 1800–1900*, (New York: Oxford University Press, 1978), pp. 3–124.

59. Roe v. Wade, 410 U.S. 117, 206–208 (1973).

60. Palko v. Connecticut, 302 U.S. 319 (1937).

Chapter 2

English Common and Statutory Law and Sodomy in American Law

"Sodomy was a criminal offense at common law and was forbidden by the laws of the original thirteen states when they ratified the Bill of Rights." This was the holding announced in a 1986 case—*Bowers v. Hardwick*, 478 U.S. 186—by the U.S. Supreme Court. The majority opinion, delivered by Justice Byron R. White, emphasized the common law standard under which claims of homosexuals would be denied. White's conclusion was underscored by the concurrence of Chief Justice Warren E. Burger who stated, "The common law of England, including its prohibition of sodomy, became the received law of Georgia and the other colonies."[1] Since English common law's writs and actions from earliest times had dealt with aspects of privacy and personhood, a case raising questions about invasion of privacy and rights of individuals against government naturally turned to the "common law . . . as a valuable tool in elucidating the meaning of liberty."[2]

The issues took the form of questions dealing with the historical development of the common law of sodomy. The justices of the U.S. Supreme Court in the 1980s used data about sodomy law in colonial and revolutionary America and its linkage to English common and statutory law. They analyzed U.S. state statutes and judicial opinions over the 200-year period following the adoption of the Constitution and Bill of Rights. From this focus they were influenced to rule in 1986 that Americans could not claim a basic common law right to engage in acts of sodomy. Attempts to expand a right of privacy under the federal constitution to include sodomy failed the test for those common law rights retained by Americans as their rights of Englishmen.[3]

SODOMY IN EARLY ENGLISH LAW

The major legal theorists of the English common law had all dealt with sodomy. As early as the thirteenth century a number of English judges had collaborated on a legal treatise known as *Fleta* in which they had identified and described the crime of sodomy and its punishment. *Fleta*'s section on sodomy stated that persons found guilty of intercourse with persons of their own gender or with animals were to be buried alive.[4] *Britton*, a legal treatise of the fourteenth century, was almost a verbatim translation.[5] One difference should be noted however. The penalty in *Fleta* was that of being buried alive; in *Britton* it was to be burned alive. Thus by the fourteenth century sodomy had been iden- tified in English legal treatises as a crime worthy of the supreme pun- ishment. Later common law authorities also identified and discussed the crime. William Lambarde's 1582 manual for justices, *Eirenarcha*, focused on sodomy as "buggery" and distinguished that which involved "man- kind" and that which involved beasts.[6] Michael Dalton's *The Countrey Justice* (1618) repeated Lambarde and stated, "Buggery committed with mankind or beast is felony without benefit of clergy." This last phrase simply meant that no exceptions to the punishment would be allowed. Claims of status or position could not exempt one from the penalty of the crime. Dalton also extended the crime of sodomy to include sex acts involving only women and he noted the similar severe penalties for rape and child molestation which were all felony crimes "without benefits of clergy."[7]

Sir Edward Coke presented a detailed treatment of the subject "Of Buggery, or Sodomy" in the *Third Part of the Institutes of the Laws of England* (1628). He defined sodomy as that "detestable and abominable sin, among Christians not to be named, committed by carnal knowledge against the ordinance of the Creator, and order of nature, by mankind with mankind, or with brute beast, or by womankind with brute beast." Coke summarized the common law authorities of *Fleta* and *Britton*, iden- tifying sodomy as a felony crime carrying a death penalty of either burying alive or burning. However, Coke noted that by the time of Richard I (1189–1199), execution was by hanging with the statute of 25 Henry VIII (1533) making the death penalty mandatory. This statue reached all accessories and anyone who "aided or abetted." Coke also interpreted the statute to include women. To justify the statute, Coke cited chapters and verses from eleven books of the Old and New Tes- taments of the Bible as authority. He also documented his definitions with two common law case precedents found in *The Mirror of Justices*,[8] an ancient set of common law judicial case precedents. The first of these was a 1608 case of homosexual child molestation and the second a case of bestiality. Coke's admirer, William Hawkins, another eminent scholar of the common law, summed up its position on sodomy this way:

All unnatural carnal copulations, whether with man or beast, seem to come under the notion of sodomy, which was felony by the ancient common law, and punished, according to some authors, with burning; according to others, ... with burying alive.[9]

Sir William Blackstone, the foremost common law authority to exert direct influence on Americans, referred to sodomy as "the infamous crime against nature," an offense of a "dark nature" and of "deep malignity." Because the crime was one "not fit to be named," English law did not describe it in the indictments. There were no exceptions to the punishment; all participants were equally guilty and subject to the death penalty.[10]

Throughout the Middle Ages in England, church courts had acted to establish and enforce biblical-based prohibitions against sodomy. King Alfred the Great in the ninth century, supporting the early medieval church's efforts to punish sodomy, listed specific reasons for opposing it. Sodomy, he said, subverted the order of nature; it was "disgusting[ly] foul"; it was "addict[ive]" and a "vice" not easily broken; it was contagious as any disease and spread rapidly." At first the state was not involved in sodomy prosecutions, and the church had the authority to deal with the crime. The medieval church's attempts to formulate a coherent policy was thwarted, however, by the conflict between those recommending a non-capital punishment and those insisting on the death penalty.

The Norman Conquest in the eleventh century increased public awareness of sodomy. One of William the Conqueror's sons, William II, was rumored to have engaged in a homosexual way of life and was denounced by leaders like the Abbot of Gloucester. After William II died in mysterious circumstances, his brother, Henry I, laid down fresh penalties for sodomy. Nevertheless, his own son was associated with the practice. During the reign of Richard the Lion Heart, 1189–1199, the penalties of hanging for men and drowning for women were prescribed for those convicted in church courts of sodomy. The church law was clear: sodomy even in secret was highly criminal and attempted sodomy was a grounds for divorce. Intense opposition to sodomy increased during the fourteenth century when Edward II, a known homosexual, became king of England. English barons were violently hostile to Edward's sexual proclivities: in 1312, the Parliament demanded that Edward exile his lover, Hugh le Despenser. Ultimately Edward was deposed, tortured, and murdered. The terrible manner of his death in 1327 and that of Hugh le Despenser demonstrated the attitude of the times.

In 1376, during the reign of Edward III, members of the English Parliament were still registering their concern with the "too horrible vice which is not to be named." Insisting that numerous foreign merchants had been encouraging sodomitical practices, the members of Parliament unsuccessfully urged the king to banish all the Lombard (Italian) merchants. However, it was not until the time of Henry VIII in 1533 that the state officially took over the punishment of the offense of sodomy. The immediate occasion for the transfer of jurisdiction over prosecution for sodomy from church courts to state court was due to England's break with the Roman Catholic Church.[11]

The 1533 statute of Henry VIII sought to reduce the jurisdiction of the church courts by withdrawing from them the right to try certain offenses—including sodomy—which were now to be regarded as secular crimes. Sodomy thus became a felony triable in the ordinary courts. The Act of 25 Henry VIII, chapter 6, was a short piece of legislation. Originating in the House of Lords, it declared the "detestable and abominable Vice of Buggery (Sodomy) committed with mankind or beast" to be a felony. The penalty was death and no exceptions were allowed. The offense was now made triable by justices of the peace, as were other felonies. The act was reenacted in 1536, 1539, and 1541. It was also reenacted under Edward VI in 1548. Under Queen Mary Tudor an attempt was made to return power to the church courts, but with the succession of Queen Elizabeth I in 1563 the statute of Henry VIII was reenacted yet again. The preamble of this reenactment stated that the "horrible and detestable vice" had increased among "divers ill disposed persons" thus forcing the state to renew its prosecutions.[12] The first recorded instance of official state action involved an author and clergyman, the Reverend Nicholas Udall and occurred in 1541.

During the late sixteenth and early seventeenth centuries actions were taken against both commoners and against the nobility.[13] The trial of Mervin Touchet, Lord Audley, Earl of Castlehaven for "Abetting a Rape on his Countess" and "Sodomy with his Servants" demonstrated that class status provided no protection.[14] Accused by his wife and his son, Castlehaven was tried by the peers of the realm in a state trial. The details of charges were considered shocking and the indictment was written in Latin instead of the customary English. The trial took place in the House of Lords in 1631, before the Lord High Steward and twenty-seven other peers with the principal judges, including Sir Nicholas Hyde, Lord Chief Justice of the Court of King's Bench also present. The prosecution was in the hands of the attorney general, Sir Robert Heath. The witnesses included Lady Castlehaven and three servants: Lawrence Fitzpatrick, Henry Skipwith, and Giles Broadway.

The attorney general stated the legal position regarding the crime of sodomy thus:

As for the *crimen sodomiticum*...it is of so abominable and vile a nature (that as the indictment truly expresses it, *crimen inter Christianos non nominandum*), it is a crime not to be named among Christians; and...by the ancient laws of England, it was punished with death. *Fleta* I.6.Cap. 35. *Sodomitae in terra vivi confodiantur*: Sodomites are to be buried alive in the earth.... The statute of 25 Henry 8. Cap. 6. made it felony without clergy revived by the 5 Elizabeth Cap. 17,...still in force.[15]

Castlehaven was convicted of sodomy and sentenced to be hanged. However, King Charles I commuted this to beheading since Castlehaven was a nobleman, and the sentence was carried out on Tower Hill on May 14, 1631. Six weeks later the servants Fitzpatrick and Broadway were tried, convicted, sentenced to death, and hanged at Tyburn. The judges stated their view that equal justice must prevail for all classes in these words:

We for our parts thought it to stand with the honour of common justice, seeing their testimony had been taken to bring a peer of the realm to his death for an offense as much theirs as his, that they should as well suffer for it as he did, lest any jealousy should arise.[16]

The law of sodomy carrying the death penalty was no "respect(er) of persons" and the trial of Lord Castlehaven remained the leading case precedent for sodomy prosecutions for almost two centuries.

Sodomy was zealously prosecuted during the period following the English Civil War and Puritan England sought to stamp it out. Even after the restoration of the monarchy in 1660, sodomy carried the death penalty; the 1700s continued this approach. Attempted sodomy was also prosecuted and courts were expected to pronounce the sentence of death. Reprieves however were sometimes possible. During one court session in 1726 five men were tried for sodomy. Four of them were found guilty; one was acquitted. Three of those convicted were hanged at Tyburn but one was reprieved. Some of those accused of sodomy fled the country rather than risk a trial. Robert Thislethwayte, a warden at Wadham College, Oxford, was brought before the local bench of magistrates in 1739 and committed for trial at the next assizes for attempted sodomy. While out on bail pending trial, he fled to France rather than stand trial.[17]

MODERN ENGLAND'S APPROACH TO SODOMY

Toward the end of the eighteenth century, legal arguments over the definition of the law of evidence to prove the crime produced two different case results. In 1777 twelve judges ruled that either the act of penetration or that of emission of semen was sufficient to convict and execute a man for the crime of sodomy. In 1781, however, the court refused to order the execution of one Hill, convicted of attempted sodomy according to only the last half of the 1777 test.[18] Attempts to commit sodomy were usually punished by pillory, and death sometimes resulted from the action of the mob as they hurled bottles and stones. In 1810 the exposure of the White Swan Homosexual Club resulted in seven men being sent to the pillory. A huge mob gathered and behaved with unusual brutality, causing severe injuries.

Sodomy continued to be a capital crime in England into the early years of the nineteenth century and judges and juries generally imposed the extreme penalty. In 1829 Parliament passed the Offenses Against the Person Act (9 George IV c.31) affirming the death penalty for sodomy and declaring that proof of the act of penetration was sufficient for conviction. The statute thus returned the law of evidence to its earlier form, and, in the words of Sir Robert Peel who proposed the measure, "re-established the ancient law of England as it [had always] existed." The statute was accepted and applied by the courts and judges in cases like *R. v. Robert Reekspear* (1832) I Mood. 342. Reekspear was executed under the 1829 statute's evidentiary requirements. In 1865 imprisonment for life or for any term not less than ten years became the new penalty for sodomy, with attempts to engage in sodomy punishable by a maximum of ten years imprisonment. The Criminal Law Amendment Act of 1885 set a penalty of two years imprisonment at hard labor for those engaging in acts of "gross indecency," short of sodomy, whether public or private.

In recent years sodomy laws have undergone major revisions. The Sexual Offenses Act of 1967 made all homosexual acts—sodomy, gross indecency, procurement—committed by men over twenty-one with youths of sixteen up to twenty-one, a crime. For sodomy or indecency with boys under sixteen the penalty remained that of life imprisonment. Homosexual acts whether of gross indecency or sodomy, committed by a youth under twenty-one with a consenting partner of any age over sixteen, incurred a penalty of up to two years' imprisonment. The freedom of those over twenty-one to indulge in acts of sodomy in private were hedged with several limitations. No act was considered legally private if more than two persons were present.[19]

SODOMY LAWS IN AMERICA: COLONIAL, REVOLUTIONARY, AND FEDERAL PERIODS

Massachusetts Bay Colony in 1641 identified sodomy as one of twelve capital crimes. Section 8 of the 1641 laws stated, "If any man lyeth with mankinde as he lyeth with a woman, both of them have committed abomination, they both shall surely be put to death." New Plymouth

Colony copied Massachusetts but added the proviso that if one party were "forced," or if one participant were under the age of fourteen, then a severe punishment could be substituted for the death penalty for that individual. After Massachusetts Bay Colony and New Plymouth joined together into one colony, a new statute was written which read as follows:

For avoiding of the detestable and abominable sin of buggery with mankind or beast, which is contrary to the very law of nature; Be it enacted ... that the same offense be adjudged felony ... and that every man, being duly convicted of lying with mankind, as he lieth with a woman: and every man or woman, that shall have carnal copulation with any beast ... shall suffer the pains of death.[20]

This provision drew for its wording on the 1533 English statute of Henry VIII. Colonial leaders like William Bradford warned colonists that they would lose the New World unless they put an end to sodomy.[21] This view paralleled that of the English attorney general, who while prosecuting the Earl of Castlehaven for sodomy, warned of divine retribution if England failed to punish sodomites.[22]

In colonial Connecticut a capital code introduced in 1642 copied the Bay Colony law and made sodomy a felony crime carrying the death penalty. The Codes of 1673, 1796, 1808, and 1822 added the words "except it appears that one of the parties were forced, or under *fifteen years* of age" to the sodomy statute. The Colony of New Haven made a detailed and rigorous analysis of the crime of sodomy and defined it to cover several types of deviant sex. Lesbianism was clearly defined and made subject to the death penalty.[23]

Colonial New Hampshire copied the New Plymouth Code of 1671. Sodomy was a capital crime but "a severe punishment" could be substituted in a case where one party was "forced" or under fourteen years of age. In 1718 and 1792 the New Hampshire colonial legislature adopted a sodomy law modeled on the Massachusetts version of the 1533 statute of Henry VIII. In the colony of Rhode Island the first law on sodomy was appended to Roger Williams's charter in 1647. It read as follows:

First of sodomy, which is forbidden by this present assembly throughout the whole colony, and by sundry statutes of England. 25 Henry 8, 6; 5 Eliz. 17. It is a vile affection. ... The penalty concluded by that state under whose authority we are is felony of death without remedy. See 5 Eliz. 17.[24]

Colonial New York, influenced first by Dutch laws, made sodomy a capital offense. In 1674 the English promulgated the "Duke of York's Code" which also imposed capital punishment.[25] This statute was regarded by the colonists in New York as applicable until after the American Revolution. On February 14, 1787, the New York state legislature passed a law explicitly enforcing the death penalty for those convicted of the crime of sodomy.

In colonial Pennsylvania William Penn's "Great Law" of December 7, 1682, identified sodomy as a crime to be punished by the state. Chapter 9 of the Code provided that "if any person shall be legally convicted of the unnatural sin of sodomy or joining with beasts, such persons shall be whipt, and forfeit one third of his or her estate, and work six months in the House of Correction at hard labour, and for the Second offense, imprisonment as aforesaid, during life."[26] This remained the law for almost twenty years in Pennsylvania. On November 27, 1700, the state assembly adopted even stricter penalties. The new Pennsylvania "Act Against Incest, Sodomy, and Bestiality" required that "whosoever shall be legally convicted of sodomy or bestiality, shall suffer imprisonment during life and be whipped at the discretion of the magistrates, once every three months during the first year after conviction. And if he be a married man, he shall also suffer castration, and the injured wife shall have a divorce if required."[27] In 1718 the following comprehensive phrasing was adopted:

If any person or persons shall commit sodomy . . . he or they . . . shall suffer as felons, according to the tenor, direction, form and effect of the several statutes in such cases made and provided in Great Britain, any act or law of this province to the contrary notwithstanding.[28]

Part of the colony of New Jersey during the late 1600s operated under the sodomy provision found in New York's "Duke of York's Code" which provided for the death penalty except in case of underaged participants or where force had been used. When East and West New Jersey were united in 1702 no new statute on sodomy was written.[29] The colony instead simply regarded the English common and statute law as being in force.

This approach was also characteristic of that used in southern colonies—Virginia, Maryland, Georgia, North Carolina, and South Carolina. At the time of the ratification of the U.S. Constitution and of the Bill of Rights, Virginia, for example, was still operating under the adopted English common law and the death penalty for sodomy was mandatory. In 1779 the Virginia legislature considered the proposal of a committee which recommended, under the influence of Thomas Jefferson, that castration and mutilation be substituted for the death penalty. However, the legislature never adopted this bill. When Virginia did issue its Criminal Code on December 10, 1792, sodomy was treated exactly as it had been under the English law: a mandatory capital felony. Maryland also operated under the English statute of 25 Henry VIII, 6. In 1776, on the eve of the Revolution, Maryland reaffirmed its intention of retaining the English common law.

Georgia's dependence on English law was clearly asserted only one year after the American Declaration of Independence was signed. On June 7, 1777, the Georgia legislature specifically adopted "all the laws of England, as well statute as common, relative to criminal matters . . . heretofore used and adopted in the courts of law in this state." This, of course, included the statutes of Henry VIII, and Elizabeth I on sodomy, as well as the English case precedents involving prosecutions and convictions for sodomy. Following the Revolution, North Carolina compiled a list of English statutes from its colonial period as the basis for law under its new status as a state. The 1792 "Collection of the Statutes of the Parliament of England in Force in North Carolina" listed the English statute of 25 Henry VIII, 6 and that of 5 Elizabeth 17; it then reprinted both English laws verbatim. South Carolina had done this earlier, reaffirming the words of the English statutes adopted in 1712.[30]

After the American Revolution and during the period when the federal Constitution and the Bill of Rights were being written and adopted, states continued to prosecute sodomy. The thirteen original colonies at the time of the adoption of the Constitution and Bill of Rights all were operating under the English common and statutory law theory that sodomy was a felony crime carrying the death penalty. How many executions actually took place is not completely documented but the threat was real: In 1785 Pennsylvania executed a man for the "crime against nature."[31]

Some states retained the death penalty for sodomy even into the early nineteenth century. Other states began to substitute lesser penalties such as imprisonment and fines. New Jersey in 1796 substituted "a fine and solitary confinement at hard labor for any term not exceeding twenty-one years" for the death penalty. New York, also in 1796, substituted life imprisonment. Rhode Island's Public Laws of 1798 prescribed the following penalty:

Every person who shall be convicted of sodomy . . . shall, for the first offence, be carried to the gallows in a cart, and set upon the said gallows, for a space of time not exceeding four hours, and thence the common goal, there to be confined for a term not exceeding three years, and shall be grievously fined at the discretion of the court; and for the second offence shall suffer death.[32]

In 1805 Massachusetts's "Act against Sodomy and Bestiality" made the penalty for these crimes imprisonment "not exceeding ten years." New Hampshire made the penalty "not less than one nor more than ten years." Georgia prescribed life imprisonment in the Penal Code of 1816 while

Delaware's Code of 1826 imposed "solitary confinement and a public whipping." North Carolina kept the death penalty for sodomy until 1869 when it was reduced to imprisonment. South Carolina retained the English statute of Henry VIII with its mandatory death penalty until 1873.[33]

SODOMY IN AMERICAN LAW: NINETEENTH- AND TWENTIETH-CENTURY COURT DECISIONS AND STATE STATUTES

In the years following the adoption of the U.S. Constitution and the Bill of Rights, the individual state legislative bodies gradually moved to create precise definitions of the criminal actions they wanted to proscribe under their state police powers. Their right to legislate in this area was based in part on their traditional power as retained under the Tenth Amendment's guarantee in the federal Constitution. In the process of seeking definitions of activities that would constitute sodomy, the state legislative bodies turned to English common law. They started with the common law's basic statement of the crime. English common and statutory law had generally avoided describing the precise acts that would constitute the crime of sodomy. Blackstone praised the wisdom of English law in its refusal to define the proscribed acts, explaining that the degrading nature of the crime was the reason why the offense should not be described in detail as were other criminal acts. Many Americans judges and legislators followed this practice. Various terms were used to identify sodomy: a "crime against nature"; "unnatural and lascivious acts"; "buggery." Courts and legislators agreed that the crime of sodomy was of such a "disgusting nature" that a description of it in detail in either a law, in a criminal indictment, or in a court opinion would constitute obscenity. Thus U.S. state legislators and judges proceeded on the theory that the term, "crime against nature," had such a well-recognized meaning that further detail was unnecessary. The sodomy statutes in the American states from earliest times contained the adjectives of censure found in early English law.[34] They also included the specific actions listed by common law authorities like Coke. Coke identified certain actions which, he believed, should be defined as sodomy: anal intercourse between humans and bestiality.

Using these as the basis for actions to be prohibited under state sodomy statutes many legislative bodies then developed an increasingly precise listing of supplementary and additional forms which sodomy might take. Homosexual acts, lesbian acts, certain acts between heterosexual partners, acts with beasts or corpses, and so on all began to be specified in many state statutes. Greater attention to detail characterized the legislative activity during the nineteenth and twentieth centuries. However, the states were not uniform in this practice: some state statutes were more precise than others. States differed among themselves concerning all of the actions they wanted to proscribe legally. Different levels of penalties were set up in the state statutes of the nineteenth and twentieth centuries. Most statutes did address factors such as the use of force, the age of the participants, and the element of public nuisance associated with the commission of the criminal act.[35]

Thus the various state statutes, by the twentieth century, emphasized different elements within the English common law of sodomy. Many state statutes continued to employ the traditional English decorous terminology and insisted that the vague wording was both necessary and appropriate. Other states, however, used more precise definitions of the exact actions including English evidentiary standards for imposing criminal sanctions. However, U.S. legislative bodies like their counterparts in England shared power with the judicial branch. Judges decided cases that gave meaning and definition to the statutory provisions enacted by the legislative bodies. And the judges, like legislators, also found themselves facing two parallel English traditions and approaches to sodomy. The vague and potentially expansive decorous language approach existed side by side with the basic but noncomprehensive listing of proscribed sexual acts to be defined as sodomy.[36]

An examination of decisions made by judicial bodies in three different states demonstrates that courts usually adopted one of these two English approaches. In 1904 a landmark decision involving sodomy was handed down by the Georgia state supreme court. The case was *Herring v. State of Georgia*, 119 Ga. 709 (1904). The question presented to the court involved a choice of English traditions. Should the court, focusing on Coke's approach, define sodomy using the basic English definition of anal intercourse between humans to limit convictions under the Georgia statute? Or, should the court allow the extension of the state statute to cover unspecified acts based on the English tradition of decorous terminology? The Georgia state supreme court opted for the latter of these choices. The Georgia court reasoned that if "the baser forms of the abominable and disgusting crime against nature—i.e., oral—had prevailed in the days of the early common law, the courts in England could well have held that that form of the offense was included in the current definition of crime of sodomy." The Georgia court then went on to state that the statute's adoption of the English decorous phrase "the abominable crime not fit to be named among Christians," could reach any of the various "means by which this crime may be committed." This precedent was followed in a 1911 case and again in a 1916 case. In the latter, case, *Jones v. State of Georgia*, 17 Ga. App. 825 (1916), the Georgia court of appeals followed the English decorous language approach and noted, "We are unwilling to soil the pages of our reports with lengthened discussion of this loathsome subject." Georgia courts continued to allow a broad construction of the state's sodomy statute and to refuse to require that the legislature detail every "unnatural act" they sought to prohibit.[37]

The state courts in North Carolina also acted within the framework of the English common law. Courts in that state were often asked to rule that sodomy in North Carolina was limited to the basic English common law definition as found in Coke, and not to allow an expanded definition based on decorous language. North Carolina legislators had adopted the phrase, "the crime against nature," and courts had to decide if the article "the" limited the crime only to the activity as it had been specifically named and actually listed by the English common law authorities. In a 1917 decision, *State of North Carolina v. Griffin*, 175 N.C. 767, the North Carolina court held that the phrase "the crime against nature" certainly included the basic English common law definition of sodomy and bestiality. In addition, however, the court also held that the phrase could be enlarged to include deviant acts not specifically mentioned by this type of interpretation. In the 1964 case of *State of North Carolina v. O'Keefe*, 236 N.C. 53, the state court held that the "ancient origin of the offense and the uniformity of practice in the courts" gave the phrase "crime against nature" a well-recognized meaning. Thus the court decided that a statute providing for the "punishment of the abominable and detestable crime against nature" was "sufficiently descriptive of a crime known to the common law."[38] It was therefore not a vague statute and hence constitutional.

When a federal district court was called upon to decide if this North Carolina sodomy statute was unconstitutional because of its vagueness, the justices affirmed the power of state courts to expand the common law definition. The federal justices stated:

If the [North Carolina] statute were a new one, it would be obviously unconstitutional for vagueness. The former concern for the feelings of those reading the statute has yielded to the necessity that an indicted person know of what he is charged. Euphemisms have no place in criminal statutes. But this is not a new statute, and it has been interpreted many times by the North Carolina Supreme Court. Although the court has said it means much more than it meant at common law or as an enactment during the reign of Henry VIII, its decisions have made it equally clear that the crime against nature does not embrace walking on the grass.[39]

A year later the North Carolina court in *State v. Harward*, 264 N.C. 746 (1965), again emphasized its intention to make the North Carolina sodomy law inclusive of all deviant activity, and found authority to do this in Blackstone. Said the court, "According to Blackstone, the English law treated the offense in its indictment as 'unfit to be named among Christians.'... Our courts are not less sensitive than their English predecessors."[40]

Courts in New Jersey by the 1950s chose to focus on the specified acts of sodomy that the English common law had clearly identified in Coke's day. In the case of *State of New Jersey v. Morrison*, 25 N.J. Super. 534 (1953), the court was asked to interpret the reach of the New Jersey sodomy statute. This act prohibited "sodomy, or the infamous crime against nature, committed with mankind or beast." In resorting to English common law to interpret the statute, the New Jersey court was guided by two primary principles: first, that "penal statutes must be strictly construed" and second, that "if a change in the common law is to be effected by statute, the legislative intent to accomplish the change must be clearly and plainly expressed."[41] According to the New Jersey court the specified acts held to constitute sodomy under English common law were anal intercourse between humans and bestiality. The New Jersey court noted that the other states had taken a broader view of the English common law. Their decision, however, was to confine the definition of sodomy to its most narrow and precise description as stated by the early English common law authorities like Coke.[42]

THE U.S. SUPREME COURT, ENGLISH COMMON LAW, AND SODOMY: *BOWERS V. HARDWICK*

English common law played a critical and decisive role in the 1986 landmark Supreme Court sodomy case, *Bowers v. Hardwick*. Michael Hardwick was charged with violating the Georgia statute criminalizing sodomy by committing that act with another adult male in the bedroom of his home. Hardwick was observed engaging in this action by a police officer who had entered Hardwick's house with a warrant charging him with "drinking in public." This warrant was later shown to have expired since Michael Hardwick had earlier appeared in court and paid the $50 fine for the public-drinking ticket. However, the eye witness testimony of the police officer who saw Hardwick's bedroom door "partially open" led to the new charge of violation of Georgia's sodomy statute. Arrested for sodomy, Hardwick could have faced a maximum prison term of twenty years. However, before the case reached trial the district attorney pulled the case from the state court's docket by refusing to present the charges to a grand jury for indictment. This refusal to prosecute did not, however, protect Hardwick from indictment at some later time before the four-year statute of limitation expired.[43] It was Hardwick and his attorney, then, who decided to pursue the matter and in federal district court brought a challenge to the constitutionality of the Georgia statute. Losing here, they carried an appeal to the federal court of appeals which did find in favor of Hardwick's privacy rights. Georgia then petitioned the U.S. Supreme Court, pointing out that this decision seemed to contradict the Supreme Court's position in *Doe v. Common-*

wealth's Attorney for the City of Richmond, 425 U.S. 901 (1976). On this basis, the U.S. Supreme Court agreed to grant the petition for certiorari and to hear the case.

As with most cases, there were a number of issues that the lower courts as well as the U.S. Supreme Court were asked to consider and decide. Legal technicalities concerning the jurisdiction and standing of the litigants were raised; questions focusing on rights of privacy and fundamental rights emerged; and the issue of state police powers and individual rights raised questions about the role and power of courts in the decision-making process.

The role that English common law could play in helping to decide these questions appeared first in the petition for certiorari filed by the attorney general of Georgia. Mr. Bowers urged the Court to address the question of whether or not Georgia's sodomy statute infringed upon fundamental constitutional rights of homosexuals. He asked the Court to do this by applying the same type of analysis that had been used in the abortion decision, *Roe v. Wade*. This analysis, as Attorney General Bowers pointed out, had begun with "a historical review of ancient attitudes and the common law and statutory laws of England and America." Bowers pointed out that it had been this analysis which had led the Court to conclude that, "at the time of the adoption of our Constitution, and through a major portion of the 19th century, . . . a 'woman enjoyed a substantially broader right to terminate pregnancy than she does in most states today'." Attorney General Bowers then presented his own assessment of common law and sodomy: sodomy, unlike abortion, had always been a crime at common law as well as under the earliest statutes, English and American. Unlike abortion, Attorney General Bowers argued, "no similar right to engage in sodomy existed at the time of the adoption of our Constitution. [Thus] . . . sodomy of any kind including that which perchance takes place in private, cannot be considered a fundamental right or implicit in the concept of ordered liberty. Such a right is not contemplated by the Constitution." The Georgia Attorney General thus urged the U.S. Supreme Court to review the *Hardwick* case and to assess historically the position of sodomy at the time of the adoption of the Constitution.[44]

As briefs were prepared to present to the Court, the debate over English common law arose again. Attorney General Bowers and his staff proceeded to develop the argument that personal rights—privacy in this case—were limited to fundamental rights which in turn, had never included sodomy. The Georgia attorney general divided his argument into three parts: (1) the status of sodomy as a crime in English common and statutory law; (2) the legal position of sodomy in Georgia during the seventeenth and eighteenth centuries; (3) those fundamental rights that are protected by the Constitution.[45]

In discussing this first point Attorney General Bowers focused on the early history of sodomy from biblical days through the period of the Roman Empire and throughout the Middle Ages. He then turned to English tradition and law and pointed out that English statutory law had criminalized sodomy as early as 1533 during the reign of King Henry VIII. In addition, the great English common law authorities, Coke and Blackstone, had both agreed that sodomy had always been a capital crime. The attorney general's brief read as follows:

In the first half of the 17th century, Lord Coke expounded upon the crimes of buggery and sodomy, noting that the "ancient authors doe conclude, that it deserveth death, *ultimum supplicium*, though they differ in the manner of punishment." Blackstone considered "the infamous crime against nature" as an offense of "deeper malignity" than rape, and an act so heinous, "the very mention of which is a disgrace to human nature," "a crime not fit to be named."[46]

Moving to his second point, the attorney general of Georgia argued that the influence of Coke and Blackstone had clearly extended to Georgia and that Georgia had officially adopted the English common law before the adoption of the federal Constitution. According to Attorney General Bowers:

Coke's *Institutes* and the *Commentaries* (by Blackstone) were studied by colonial lawyers in America. The popularity of Coke in the colonies and the significance of that popularity was recognized by this court in *Payton v. New York*, 445 U.S. 573, 594 n. 36 (1980). Two thousand five hundred copies of the *Commentaries* were sold in America before the Revolution. . . . In Georgia, the common law of England in force prior to May 14, 1776, was adopted as the law of the state by an act of the General Assembly approved February 25, 1784. . . . In 1816, the crimes of sodomy and bestiality were made punishable in Georgia by life imprisonment at hard labor and have continuously been statutory crimes ever since.[47]

The third argument of the attorney general was designed to convince the Court that sodomy was never one of the fundamental rights of Englishmen and could not therefore "emanate from the penumbras of the First, Fourth, Fifth, and Ninth Amendments, and the concept of liberty embodied in the Fourteenth Amendment." The issue here went directly to the question of whether the "right of privacy" as articulated by earlier Supreme Courts included the right to engage in consensual homosexual sodomy. In addressing this point the Georgia attorney general argued that the historical view of the Supreme Court had been that the guarantee of personal privacy extended only to those "personal rights that can be deemed fundamental or implicit in the concept of ordered liberty." Thus unless sodomy could be shown to have been a "fundamental" right, it would not be protected under a claim of "privacy." According to the attorney general:

While the right of privacy may have its aegis in the penumbras of the Bill of Rights or the due process clause of Fourteenth Amendment, there must, at some point, be some basis for cataloging a particular activity under the protection of that right. No such basis exist for adding the crime of sodomy to the list of fundamental rights thus far recognized by the court.[48]

The attorney general reminded the Court of rights which had been deemed to be "fundamental" or implicit in the concept of ordered liberty: marriage, child bearing, child rearing, and education. These rights had been articulated by earlier courts in a number of cases. Sodomy, on the other hand was an "activity which for hundreds of years, if not thousands, ..." was condemned as immoral, and not "a legal tradition of our society." Thus sodomy failed the tests for fundamental right status. In conclusion, the Georgia attorney general argued, "Sodomy is not now and has never been a right, fundamental or statutory, in existence to be 'retained by the people' under the Ninth Amendment. Nor can it be said that sodomy was considered to be an unenumerated but inherent liberty recognized at the time the Fourteenth Amendment became part of the law of this land. It is not a part of our traditional values or conventional morality."[49]

In an attempt to undercut these arguments, Professor Laurence Tribe of Harvard Law School argued on behalf of Michael Hardwick that the right of privacy asserted in the case involved the private home. Tribe identified this right as a fundamental one, part of ordered liberty, and embedded in American tradition since the origins of the Republic.[50] Since Hardwick's action had taken place inside his home, Professor Tribe could make an appeal to additional concepts raised in the *amici curiae* brief submitted by the attorneys general of New York and California.[51] This brief had urged the Court to focus on the place where the crime and had been committed as opposed to the act itself. The legal authorities in New York and California reminded the Court that respect for privacy zones was not of recent origin but was well accepted in pre-Revolutionary English statute and common law. The focus on English precedent continued as the attorneys general quoted from Coke, from the case of *Semayne* (King's Bench, 1603), from the 1628 English *Petition of Right*. Their *amici curiae* brief noted:

More than a century before the American Revolution, Sir Edward Coke pronounced that "a man's house is his castle, and one's home is to every man the safest refuge," repeating dicta from the King's bench in *Semayne's case*, 77 Eng. Rep. 194–6 (K.B.1603), that "the House of everyone is to him his Castle and Fortress, as well for his Defence against Injury and Violence, as for his Repose."

William Pitt was inspired to his immortal statement of principle, "The poorest man in his cottage may bid defiance to all the force of the crown. It may be frail; its roof may shake; the wind may blow through it; the storms may enter; the rain may enter—but the King of England cannot enter; all his forces dare not cross the threshold of the ruined tenement!"[52]

In conclusion, these attorneys general argued that the constitutional right to be let alone had its origins in the common law tradition and they appealed to the Supreme Court to use the shield of privacy from governmental instrusion to protect private consensual sexual conduct.

Another major line of argument developed by counsel for Hardwick's position involved a nonhistorical approach, however. Noting that Western history had disapproved of homosexuality, counsel for Hardwick argued that tradition and historical approaches should not be allowed to govern the present. Quoting from the Court's opinion in *Tennessee v. Garner*, 105 S.Ct. 1694, 1703 (1985), counsel urged the Court to remember that, "Even the 'pure[st]' of '*common* law *pedigree[s]*' cannot ensure the continuing constitutional validity of long-practiced invasions of body or home." Moreover in a 1980 case, *Payton v. New York*, the Court had observed that the tradition of sanctity of the home had been deemed more important than the English common law's apparent acceptance of "warrantless entries to make felony arrests."[53]

The reply brief filed by the attorney general of Georgia urged the Court to continue to examine history and traditions carefully. Attorney General Bowers argued that the Court had always emphasized its obedience to history in deciding whether activities were protected from governmental regulation under the right of privacy. Second, he noted that in *Payton* the Court had demanded an answer to the question, "What did the common law hold at the time the Fourth Amendment was adopted?" This, Bowers argued, demonstrated the Court's reliance on English common law precedent. Finally, the attorney general urged the justices not to abandon the historical analysis previously used to identify fundamental rights. Criticizing the gay rights litigants for ignoring the historical position of sodomy at common law, the Georgia attorney general concluded:

Without history, the line drawn by the Court's previous privacy decisions might be difficult to comprehend and Respondent's difficulties may stem from his having left history outside the door. As the Court has repeatedly said . . . , "only personal rights that can be deemed 'fundamental' or 'implicit in the concept of ordered liberty,' . . . are included in this guarantee of personal privacy." *Roe v. Wade*, 410 U.S. at 152. Our history supports the view that matters involving marriage, family and child bearing should be free from state regulation. But our history does not support any "right to engage in sexual intimacy as such." It does not observe any right to engage in sodomy or sexual intimacy such as adultery, fornication incest, or bestiality. Respondent may not like these historical facts ... but this is our history."[54]

THE BOWERS DECISION: MAJORITY OPINION AND MINORITY PROTEST

These arguments about English common and statutory law appeared in the majority opinion of the U.S. Supreme Court in *Bowers v. Hardwick*. The Court in a vote of five to four, upheld the state's police power claim and appealed to the legal history of the common law for justification. Justice Byron R. White wrote the opinion for the court majority composed of Chief Justice Warren E. Burger, Justice Lewis F. Powell, Justice William H. Rehnquist, and Justice Sandra Day O'Connor. Chief Justice Warren E. Burger wrote a short, separate concurrence to underscore his agreement and to emphasize historical facts. Justice Lewis F. Powell concurred separately because he could not find an Eighth Amendment argument demonstrating cruel and unusual punishment in the case. This being so, he noted, he could not say that "conduct condemned for hundreds of years has now become a fundamental right." The four justices in dissent were Justice Harry A. Blackmun, Justice William J. Brennan, Justice Thurgood Marshall, and Justice John Paul Stevens. Justice Blackmun wrote the major dissent of nine pages, with Justice Stevens also writing a three-page dissent. The majority and the minority both used the English common law, yet differently in order to reach opposite conclusions.

Justice Byron R. White framed the central issue so as to pit history against the claims of gay rights activists. He asked, "Does the Federal Constitution confer a fundamental right upon homosexuals to engage in sodomy and hence invalidate the laws of many states that still make such conduct illegal and have done so for a very long time?" Is it not "facetious" to claim—given the historical background of criminalized sodomy—"that a right to engage in such conduct is 'deeply rooted in this nation's history and tradition' or 'implicit in the concept of ordered liberty?' " For Justice White and the other justices in the majority the answer was self-evident. There had never been a "fundamental right to engage in homosexual sodomy."

Stating that "proscriptions against (sodomy) have ancient roots," White organized the common law history of sodomy into two major sections. He began his analysis by examining American state laws at the time of the adoption of the Constitution in order to show that "sodomy was a criminal offense at common law and was forbidden by the laws of the original thirteen states when they ratified the Bill of Rights." Focusing on the year 1791, White analyzed the laws of Connecticut, Delaware, Georgia, Maryland, Massachusetts, New Hampshire, New Jersey, New

York, North Carolina, Pennsylvania, Rhode Island, South Carolina, and Virginia. In each of these states White ascertained the earliest date on which a sodomy statute had been enacted. He also documented the states who had acted "under English common law" and those that had by statute adopted the English statutory laws of Henry VIII and his successors. White noted that the state of Georgia had "adopted the Common Law of England as the law of Georgia in 1784" and that "sodomy was a crime at common law." Likewise, Maryland had claimed that her inhabitants were "entitled to the common law of England," and that "sodomy was a crime at common law." In New Jersey, White observed, "Sodomy was a crime at common law . . . at the time of the ratification of the Bill of Rights." North Carolina also "at the time of ratification of the Bill of Rights had adopted the English statute of (Henry VIII) outlawing so-domy." Although Virginia "had no specific statute outlawing sodomy . . . at the time of the ratification of the Bill of Rights, (she) had adopted the English common law" which made sodomy a capital crime.

Justice White then turned to the 1860s when the Fourteenth Amend-ment was added to the federal Constitution. Since the Supreme Court had used the Fourteenth Amendment to make the provision and guar-antees of the Bill of Rights apply against state action, this was an ap-propriate and important focus. The question now became, "What was the status of sodomy when states ratified the Fourteenth Amendment in 1868?" Justice White's investigation demonstrated that, "In 1868, when the Fourteenth Amendment was ratified, all but 5 of the 37 states in the Union had criminal sodomy laws." White noted that until 1961 all fifty states outlawed sodomy. Thus White came to his conclusion:

Against this background, to claim that a right to engage in such conduct is "deeply rooted in this nation's history and tradition" or implicit in the concept of ordered liberty" is at best facetious.[55]

Chief Justice Burger's supporting concurrence repeated White's em-phasis on the "ancient roots" of the proscriptions against sodomy and added to White's historical data. The Chief Justice noted that, "[d]uring the English Reformation . . . powers of the ecclesiastical courts were trans-ferred to the King's Court [and] the first English statute criminalizing sodomy was passed. 25 Henry VIII. C. 6." Chief Justice Burger cited Blackstone and the English common law authorities, and linked these to the state of Georgia's statutes and precedents. Burger repeated Black-stone's description of sodomy as " 'the infamous crime against nature' . . . [and] an offense of 'deeper malignity' than rape, an 'heinous act' the very mention of which is a disgrace to human nature and 'a crime not fit to be named.' Blackstone's commentaries 215." Blackstone, the Chief Justice emphasized, was identifying the status of sodomy in "the common law of England"; it was prohibited. And it was this "common law of England, including its prohibition of sodomy (which) became the received law of Georgia and the other Colonies." Thus Chief Justice Burger concluded that, "To hold that the act of homosexual sodomy is somehow protected as a fundamental right would be to cast aside millenia of moral teaching."[56]

For the justices in the minority it became important to prove two theses: first, to show that standards evolved and as a result the past could not be allowed to bind the present; and second, to demonstrate that sodomy laws were so rooted in religious beliefs as to create an establishment of religion in violation of the First Amendment. Justice Blackmun sought authority for abandoning historical practices in a quote from *The Path of the Law* by Justice Oliver W. Holmes, Jr., saying, "It is revolting to have no better reason for a rule of law than that so it was laid down in the time of Henry VIII. It is still more revolting if the grounds upon which it was laid down have vanished long since, and the rule simply persists from blind imitation of the past."

Blackmun emphasized his belief that Georgia's sodomy statute was grounded in religious tradition. He noted that the attorney general of Georgia had appealed for support to traditional Judeo-Christian values by quoting from the Old and New Testaments and the writings of St. Thomas Aquinas. Conformity to religious doctrine worked against a valid invocation of state power. "Thus," said Justice Blackmun, "far from buttressing his case, petitioner's[57] invocation of Leviticus, Romans, St. Thomas Aquinas, and sodomy's heretical status during the Middle Ages undermines his suggestions that [the Georgia statute] represents a legitimate use of secular coercive power." Justice Blackmun also tied English common law into church law in the following passage:

The theological nature of the origin of Anglo-American antisodomy statutes is patent. It was not until 1533 that sodomy was made a secular offense in England, 25 Henry VIII, Cap. 6. Until that time, the offense was, in Sir James Stephen's words, "merely ecclesiastical." 2 J. Stephen, *A History of the Criminal Law of England* 430 (1883). Pollock and Maitland similarly observed that "[t]he crime against nature . . . was so closely connected with heresy that the vulgar had but one name for both." 2 F. Pollock & F. Maitland, *The History of English Law* 544 (1895). The transfer of jurisdiction over prosecution for sodomy to secular courts seems primarily due to the alteration of ecclesicastical jurisdiction attendant on England's break with the Roman Catholic Church, rather than to any new understanding of the sovereign's interest in preventing or punishing the behavior involved. Cf. E. Coke, *The Third Part of the Institutes of the Laws of England*, ch. 10 (4th ed. 1797).[58]

Thus Blackmun concluded that sodomy laws could be attacked as establishing certain religious views in violation of the First Amendment.

Justice Stevens had two principal points. First, he suggested that the state of Georgia was applying the common law concept of sodomy selectively. Second, he believed that historical tradition alone was insufficient justification for prohibiting totally certain kinds of conduct. Stevens noted that while the court majority had focused on homosexual sodomy, English common law condemned heterosexual as well as homosexual sodomy and reached married couples' behavior. Stevens cited William Hawkins's *Pleas of the Crown* which defined sodomy as "all unnatural carnal copulations, whether with man or beast." Noting that Blackstone had described sodomy as a crime "committed either with man or beast," Justice Stevens then cited E. H. East, a later common law authority. In 1803 East had defined sodomy in his *Pleas of the Crown* as "carnal knowledge committed against the order of nature by man with man, or in the same unnatural manner with woman, or by man or woman in any manner with beast." This definition had been repeated, Stevens noted in J. Hawley and M. McGregor's *The Criminal Law* which had stated:

Sodomy is the carnal knowledge against the order of nature by two persons with each other, or of a human being with a beast.
... The offense may be committed between a man and a woman, or between two male persons, or between a man or a woman and a beast.[59]

An American common law scholar of the nineteenth century, Justice J. May, had stated that sodomy could be committed "by a man with a woman—his wife, in which case, if she consents, she is an accomplice." For Stevens all of this "history of the statutes cited by the majority as proof for the proposition that sodomy in not constitutionally protected, similarly reveals a prohibition on heterosexual as well as homosexual sodomy." This traditional view of sodomy as an immoral kind of conduct regardless of the identity of the persons who engaged in it raised questions about actual prosecutions under the Georgia statute. If Georgia applied the statute selectively, its constitutionality would clearly be in jeopardy.

Stevens agreed with Justice Blackmun that standards evolved over time, that the past should not constrain the present, and stated that "the fact that a governing majority in a state has traditionally viewed a particular practice as immoral is not a sufficient reason for upholding a law prohibiting the practice; neither history nor tradition could save a law prohibiting miscegination from constitutional attack."[60]

CONCLUSION

What role had English common and statutory law actually played in the outcome of *Bowers v. Hardwick*? Some court analysts were surprised at the prominence given by the Court majority to these historical English roots. During the oral argument the justices had quickly pushed aside these points when introduced by Mr. Michael E. Hobbs, assistant attorney general for the state of Georgia. Mr. Hobbs had opened his argument with the statement that the case "presented the question of whether or not there is a *fundamental right* under the Constitution of the United States to engage in consenusal private homosexual sodomy." He had planned to identify fundamental rights using the historical approach grounded in English common and statutory law. However, before the attorney general was able to do this, he was inundated with questions of a different focus. The justices asked about the facts of the case, about the procedures involved; about the scope and limits of the Georgia statute as applied; about asserted powers and interests of the state. Opposing counsel, Professor Laurence H. Tribe, did not focus on the issue of fundamental rights and the questions directed to him from the bench revolved around appropriate judicial tests such as the level of scrutiny which the Court should apply in the case.

Some early predictions had suggested that the Court would split five to four, but believed it would be in favor of, rather than against, Michael Hardwick. The surprise vote was that of Justice Lewis F. Powell: Powell shifted during the course of the deliberations. His shift seemed to be influenced by the legal history, and "ancient roots" arguments identifying fundamental rights and dominating the White-Burger approach. This argument had stressed the historical analysis that the Court had previously used to identify fundamental rights. In fact, Justice Powell himself in a 1977 case, *Moore v. City of East Cleveland*, 431 U.S. 494, had identified history and tradition as a pedigree guide to the identification of fundamental rights. This approach tied back into early Court precedents as summarized in *Palko v. Connecticut*, 302 U.S. 319, 325 (1937). Justice Powell, in *Moore*, had agreed that fundamental rights had to be "deeply rooted in this nation's history and traditions."

Apparently Powell had at first joined the liberal justices in *Bowers* to strike down the Georgia law, and had so voted in the conference. However, as draft opinions circulated Powell changed his mind and his vote.[61] In his short concurrence in which he joined the White-Burger opinion, he observed in a footnote, "I cannot say that conduct condemned for hundreds of years has now become a fundamental right."[62] The Court's focus utilizing the English roots of American legal thought to define what did and did not make a right fundamental was critical for Justice Powell. Sodomy failed the test.

NOTES

1. Bowers v. Hardwick, 478 U.S. 186, 192 (1986).
2. Laurence H. Tribe, *American Constitutional Law* (Mineola, NY: The Foundation Press, 1978), p. 895.

3. Bowers v. Hardwick, 478 U.S. 196 (1986).

4. H. G. Richardson and G. O. Sayles, eds., *Fleta*, I, 35 (London: Quaritch, 1955), p. 90.

5. Francis Nichols, ed., *Britton*, vol. 1, Bk. 1 (Oxford: Clarendon, 1865), Chap. 10 (9). See also John Boswell, *Christianity, Social Tolerance, and Homosexuality* (Chicago: University of Chicago Press, 1980), p. 292.

6. William Lambarde, *Eirenarcha, or Of The Office of the Justices ofPeace* (London; 1610), pp. 224–25.

7. Michael Dalton, *The Countrey Justice*, (New York: Arno Press Reprint, 1972), pp. 340–41.

8. Edward Coke, *The Third Part of the Institutes of the Laws of England* (London: E&R Brooke, 1797), pp. 58–59.

9. William Hawkins, *Treatise of the Pleas of the Crown*, vol. 1 (1716).

10. William Blackstone, *Commentaries on the Laws of England*, vol. 4 (Birmingham, AL: Gryphon Legal Classics, 1983), pp. 215–16.

11. D. S. Bailey, *Homosexuality in the Western Christian Tradition* (Hamden, CT: Archon, 1975), pp. 100, 119, 123, 126–27, 170.

12. Sir James F. Stephen, *History of the Criminal Law of England*, 3 vols. (London: Macmillan, 1883), pp. 429–30.

13. H. Montgomery Hyde, *The Love That Dared Not Speak Its Name: A Candid History of Homosexuality in Britain* (Boston: Little, Brown, 1970), pp. 37–43.

14. Caroline Bingham, "Seventeenth-Century Attitudes Toward Deviant Sex," 1 *Journal of Interdisciplinary History* (Spring 1971), pp. 448–68.

15. "The Trial and Condemnation of Mervyn Lord Audley, Earl of Castlehaven ... for ... committing sodomy ... ," *State Trials*, vol. 3 W. Cobbett and T. Howell, eds., (London, 1909), pp. 401–25.

16. Ibid. See also Bingham, "Seventeenth-Century Attitudes Toward Deviant Sex." Bingham's account is based on the original manuscripts preserved in the Harleian Collection in the British Museum.

17. *Select Trials at the Sessions-House in the Old Bailey 1720–1742*, vol. 3 (London: Applebee, 1742; Garland Publishing Co. Reprint, 1985), pp. 37–38.

18. Hyde, *The Love That Dared Not Speak*, pp. 68–69.

19. Ibid.

20. *Acts and laws, passed by the great and general council of assembly of the province of Massachusetts Bay in New England from 1692 to 1719* (London: J. Bashelt, 1724).

21. William Bradford, *History of Plymouth Plantation*, vol. 2 (Boston: Houghton Mifflin, 1912), pp. 309, 323.

22. "Trial of the Earl of Castlehaven ... ", Howell, *State Trials*, vol. 3, pp. 401–25.

23. Quoted in Louis Crompton, "Homosexuals and the Death Penalty in Colonial America," 1 *Journal of Homosexuality* (1976), pp. 280–81.

24. W. R. Staples, ed., *Proceedings of the first general assembly of the incorporation of Providence Planation and the code of laws adopted in 1647* (Providence: Charles Bunett, 1847), pp. 31–32.

25. G. Staughton et. al., *Charter of William Penn and Laws of the Commonwealth of Pennsylvania ... preceded by Duke of York's laws* (Harrisburg: Lane S. Hart, 1879), p. 14.

26. Ibid., p. 110.

27. J. T. Mitchell and H. Flanders, eds., *The statutes at large of Pennsylvania from 1682 to 1801*, vol. 3 (Harrisburg: Clarence Busch, 1896), p. 8.

28. Ibid., vol. 3, p. 202.

29. Quoted in Crompton, "Homosexuals and the Death Penalty, p. 284.

30. Ibid.

31. Ibid., p. 288.

32. Ibid., p. 287.

33. Ibid., p. 288.

34. Robert J. Evans et al., Note: "The Crime Against Nature," 16 *Journal of Public Law* (1967), pp. 159–63.

35. Karl M. Bowman, "A Psychiatric Evaluation of Laws of Homosexualtiy," 29 *Temple Law Quarterly* (1956), pp. 273–81.

36. Note, "The Crime Against Nature," p. 163.

37. Ibid., pp. 163–66.

38. Ibid., pp. 167–69.

39. Craven, J. in Perkins v. North Carolina, 234 F. Supp. 333, 336 (W.D.W.C. 1964).

40. Note, "The Crime Against Nature," pp. 168–69.

41. Ibid., pp. 169–70.

42. State v. Morrison, 25 N. J. Super. 534, 539 (1953).

43. Peter Irons, *The Courage of Their Convictions* (New York: Penguin, 1990), pp. 381–403.

44. Petition for a Writ of Certiorari to the U.S. Ct. of Appeals for the 11th Circuit Brief of Petitioner Michael J. Bowers Attorney of Georgia, Dec. 19, 1985, pp. 310–403.

45. Ibid.

46. Ibid., pp. 382–83.

47. Ibid., p. 385–86.

48. Ibid., p. 383.

49. Ibid., pp. 388–89.

50. Brief for Respondent in Bowers v. Hardwick, Laurence H. Tribe, Counsel of Record, Jan. 31, 1986, pp. 404–39.

51. Brief of the Attorney General of the State of New York, joined by the Attorney General of the State of California, As *Amici Curiae* In Support of Respondents, pp. 552–73.

52. Ibid., pp. 563–64.

53. Brief for Respondents,... Laurence H. Tribe, Counsel of Record, pp. 418–19.

54. Reply Brief of Petitioner Michael J. Bowers, Attorney General of Georgia, March 21, 1986, pp. 440–62.

55. Bowers v. Hardwick, 478 U.S. 186, 194 (1986).

56. Ibid., p. 197.

57. Petitioner here meant the attorney general of Georgia, Michael J. Bowers.

58. Bowers v. Hardwick, 478 U.S. 186, 211–212 (1986). See Justice Blackman's note 6.

59. J. Hawley and M. McGregor, *The Criminal Law*, 3rd ed. (1899), p. 287.

60. Bowers v. Hardwick, 478 U.S. 186, 216 (1986).

61. *Washington Post,* July 13, 1986, pp. A–1, A–8. See also Irons, *The Courage of Their Convictions*, pp. 381–403.

62. Bowers v. Hardwick, 478 U.S. 198 (1986). See Justice Powell's Concurrence, note 2.

Chapter 3 ─────────────────────────────

Pornography: English Precedents in American Legal Thought

Defining obscenity/pornography has long been a perplexing task for Anglo-American decision makers. Scholars, clergymen, legislators, judges, and juries have all struggled with this problem. In the United States one of the earliest definitions was handed down by judges in the 1821 case of *Commonwealth of Massachusetts v. Peter Holmes.*[1] Peter Holmes, a printer and publisher, was charged with publishing an English novel, John Cleland's *Memoirs of a Woman of Pleasure* or *Fanny Hill*. The indictment described the book as "lewd and obscene." In finding Peter Holmes guilty, the court used three criteria for obscenity. First, the publication was designed to "debauch and corrupt the morals of youth as well as other good citizens." Second, it constituted a disturbance of the peace. Finally, the publisher's intent in publishing was "evil." The right and power of American courts to render such a judgment was also at issue as the Massachusetts court linked its power and jurisdiction to that of the English courts of quarter sessions. These courts had often decided cases of obscene libel. Having articulated tests for obscenity and asserted jurisdiction, the judges on the Massachusetts court in 1821 sentenced Peter Holmes to a jail term, a fine of $300, court costs of $75.53, and a $500 bond for good behavior in the future.

The American judges who decided that *Holmes* case based their definition of obscenity on a 1727 English precedent, *Rex v. Curll*. Moreover, their decision and actions reflected that of English authorities in 1749 who launched a series of legal actions against this same publication— John Cleland's *Memoirs of Pleasure* (*Fanny Hill*). The history of the legal actions taken against this particular book in both England and the United States demonstrates the role of English precedent in American judicial efforts to define obscenity/pornography, to devise a test for recognizing and labelling a pornographic book, and to identify a proper defense. The legal history of *Memoirs* spans the period from 1749–1966, with two main proceedings occurring in England (in 1749 and in 1964) and two in the United States (in 1821 and in 1966). An analysis of these proceedings including their historic legal foundation and their contemporary modifications can provide a standard of meaning for the terms "obscenity" and "pornography." It can illustrate the significance of the English roots of American legal thought in the litigation of a moral issue such as pornography.

PORNOGRAPHY IN ENGLAND: EARLY PRECEDENTS

In early English legal history publication of "bawdy" books was dealt with by church courts as a religious offense. Although bawdy books had appeared in England before the fifteenth century, they did not come under attack until later, and there was no attempt on the part of the state to identify and control this literature until the sixteenth century. Secular courts and legislators undertook this task only after advances in printing created a flood of inexpensive books and pamphlets. Judges, kings, and Parliament would ultimately interact to establish definitions and create controls: kings and Parliament did this through the Licensing Act of 1533 and its progeny; English secular courts assumed responsibility in the 1727 case of *Rex v. Curll*.[2]

This case focused on Edmund Curll, an enterprising London book publisher and seller, who, by the 1720s had acquired considerable notoriety through the printing and selling of translations of bawdy French works. He had also printed scandal sheets focusing on the private lives of the English aristocracy and clergy. Curll had gained access to secrets of those in political office; he himself had actually worked as a secret informer for the government. However, Curll had little success as a spy, and his overbold printing of scandalous and unauthorized works caused the House of Lords to summon him twice before them for reprimand. In late 1724 he was arrested for publishing an obscene book and during the next four years he was in and out of prison with his case pending before the Court of King's Bench. Curll pleaded innocent of any crime. His attorney questioned the jurisdiction of the common law courts and quoted a precedent, *Regina v. Read*, (1708), in which the secular courts had thrown out a case involving publication of material charged with corrupting good manners on the grounds that church courts had jurisdiction.[3] However, the attorney general argued that Curll's books were indeed punishable at common law because they tended to corrupt the morals of the king's subjects and were an offense against the peace of the king in that they might incite a riot. As the argument proceeded in court, the Lord Chief Justice suggested a standard that could settle the jurisdictional argument: "if it (the publication) reflects on religion, virtue or morality . . . [and] tends to disturb the civil order of society." This approach would allow common law courts to have power over all cases which involved obscene publications. Although the other justices agreed that they all knew offensive material when they saw it, they still could not agree on why it was a libel. Neither could they agree on grounds for claiming jurisdiction. Thus they delayed judgment in *Rex v. Curll.*

Meanwhile, Curll languished in prison. When finally allowed out on bail he immediately created new problems by publishing three volumes of the memoirs of an ex-government agent and fellow prisoner, John Ker. Ker had written about the "villainy and vanity" that pervaded the political world, and Curll's determination to place this material in the hands of the reading public landed him back in jail with an additional charge. The government now charged that unauthorized publication of a government agent's activities constituted seditious libel.

At length the justices of the Court of King's Bench reached a decision in Curll's case and established two major rules. First, common law courts like King's Bench were now identified as the proper forum for adjudicating questions about obscene publications; second, an obscene libel was specifically defined as material that corrupted the "morals of the King's subjects" and was "against the peace of the King." Under these new standards Curll was convicted and fined fifty marks; he was also required to post a bond of one hundred pounds for a year's good behavior. In addition, dicta used by the attorney general during the prosecution made it possible to argue that not only obscene books, but also books critical of government and religion, could all be suppressed under the umbrella charge of being "destructive of the King's Peace."[4]

The fact that seditious libel and religious blasphemy were linked to an obscenity prosecution in this case would later raise problems and questions for American jurists. Was this case precedent, ostensibly dealing with an obscene publication, really a cover for reaching a printer critical of the government? In the 1730s and 1740s, however, English officials only used this precedent to justify warrants against books which they believed corrupted the morals of the king's subjects. Even though legal actions against undesirable printing were not common events in eighteenth-century England, Curll's case indicated that individuals could be successfully prosecuted in civil courts. A network of agents known as "Messengers to the Press" were charged with discovering and reporting to the secretary of state books considered destructive of morality. They were also authorized to seize not only the book but also the author, printer, and publisher and to detain them indefinitely.[5]

A CASE STUDY IN PROSECUTION OF PORNOGRAPHY: MEMOIRS OF A WOMAN OF PLEASURE—ACT ONE, EIGHTEENTH-CENTURY ENGLAND

The legal background for prosecution of materials deemed to be "obscene libel" existed within the parameters established by *Curll* when John Cleland, imprisoned for debt and angry with the social-economic world of the eighteenth century, produced the novel destined to become the "prima ballerina" of pornography. *The Memoirs of a Woman of Pleasure*, appeared in two separate volumes in 1748 and 1749. In November 1749, nine months after the second volume had been advertised and almost one year to the day of publication of the first volume, the government issued warrants for all the principals involved in the writing, publishing, and distribution of this "obscene" book. *Memoirs* was identified as a publication that corrupted the morals of the king's subjects and was detrimental to social order and peace. The legal proceedings that followed would indicate the author, publisher, and printer of *Memoirs* all experienced punitive measures against their persons and possessions. Some eight legal actions against *Memoirs* occurred between 1749–1750 and none of the principals involved escaped unscathed. The first action came in the form of a warrant issued by the secretary of state in response to the complaint of religious leaders. The warrant ordered the seizure of John Cleland (author), Ralph Griffiths (printer), and Thomas Parker (publisher). Cleland was taken to the house of the arresting officer and required to give a full account of his part in producing *Memoirs*. At the same time Griffiths was required to appear before the secretary of state's law clerk for the same purpose. Ultimately Cleland secured his own release by posting a one-hundred pound bond. Griffiths and Parker also had to post similar bonds. They all promised to appear when summoned to the Court of King's Bench.

While awaiting this summons, Cleland and Griffiths produced a revised edition of *Memoirs* which they called *Fanny Hill* and from which they removed anything which they thought could lead to legal charges. Griffiths published this new edition four months later. However, it not only failed to get the charges removed, it actually led to a new charge for publishing the revised edition. Thus a fifth legal proceeding—a new warrant—was entered upon the record, which now included the initial detention warrant, the official confinement action, the deposition or statement, and the bond/bail proceedings. Cleland was again taken into custody and all copies of the book were seized and confiscated. Griffiths and Cleland for a second time were examined by officials and then released on their initial bond which the authorities still held.[6]

Meanwhile the secretary of state began pressuring the attorney general for immediate prosecution of Cleland, Griffiths, and Parker on both the old and the new charges of writing, publishing, and selling the first edition and the revised edition of an obscene book. Feeling was running high in certain influential circles in London. Two earthquakes had shaken the city in the early months of 1750, and the second one had occurred the very day the revised edition of *Memoirs* appeared. The bishop of London, Thomas Sherlock, had been crusading against "bawdy books" and he wrote the secretary of state urging that "this vile book" be stopped. The coincidence of the publication of the revised edition of *Memoirs* and the occurrence of the second earthquake—both on March 8, 1750—allowed Sherlock to suggest that it was divine retribution for publishing these "histories or romances of the vilest prostitutes." Ultimately, the issue was shelved through tacit compromises. *Memoirs* joined a growing number of books suppressed as obscene publications, but further prosecution of Cleland, Griffiths, and Parker was not pursued by the government. Periodically, others who trafficked in the books would be fined.[7]

AMERICAN PORNOGRAPHY STANDARDS: 1660s–1880s

The standards that would be used to define obscenity and provide for its control in the United States evolved from these English precedents and actions. Early American law, like English law, focused at first on political and religious printing through penalties for acts of sedition and blasphemy. Nevertheless, early colonists also moved against printed matter that "corrupted morals and created a breach of the peace." When such appeared in America—and they did appear at least as early as 1668—Americans used licensing requirements with fines as penalties to control materials deemed obscene. Sometimes offenders were easily located and dealt with as in the case of New York City bookseller, Benjamin Gomez, who was fined in 1798 for selling illustrated copies of John Cleland's *Memoirs*.[8] At other times publications circulated surreptitiously and publishers were not caught or prosecuted. Such was the case with a Massachusetts publisher, Isaiah Thomas, who published *Memoirs* clandestinely sometime between 1786 and 1814.[9] When the U.S. Constitution and Bill of Rights were drafted and adopted, they contained no mention of obscenity and the states likewise had no specific statutes aimed at obscenity as such. The first specific state obscenity laws began appearing in the 1820s with enactments by Vermont (1821), Connecticut (1834), and Massachusetts (1835). However, there had been earlier legal actions conducted without appeal to statutory provisions. The common law crimes of corrupting morals and creating a breach of the peace were used as a basis for American state prosecutions of materials deemed obscene even in the absence of specific legislative enactments against obscenity. Such was the basis for the first full-scale legal prosecution of an obscene book in the United States—Massachusetts's action against Cleland's *Memories of a Woman of Pleasure* in 1821. Lacking a specific state law against obscenity, the Massachusetts court found power to suppress *Memoirs* by convicting its American publisher, Peter Holmes, of several old English common law crimes: tending to "corrupt the morals" of youth; "wicked intent of author and publisher"; "disturbing the peace."[10]

English judges in 1646 had allowed suppression of a book entitled *The Woman's Parliament* because of its tendency to "corrupt youth." The intent of the author and publisher had appeared as English criteria as early as 1643 in a case involving an anti-Catholic publication and had been deemed a relevant standard for an obscenity charge. Moreover, the legal actions taken against John Cleland and the publishers of *Memoirs* in 1749 in England had all stressed "intent" as a legal criteria for prosecution of obscenity. The charge of "disturbing the peace" was the oldest criterion used in obscenity proceedings. In 1663 Sir Charles Sedley was prosecuted in London for obscene conduct which caused a "breach of the King's Peace." His appearing nude on a London balcony and hurling bottles containing urine upon a crowd led to legal charges against Sir Charles. The courts held that his actions had occurred *vi et armis* or with "force and arms."[11] This was the common law term for a disturbance of the peace that could be prosecuted by the government. All of these precedents were well known in the United States; in the 1821 Massachusetts case against the publisher of *Memoirs* the very same charge levied against Sir Charles Sedley was used. Publisher Peter Holmes was indicted and convicted for publishing "with force and arms" material that was "offending, and against the peace." In both cases the underlying theory was that the action might anger or annoy observers, inciting them to riot or engage in disruptive conduct, and leading to destruction of property and injury to the populace.

Following this first U.S. prosecution for obscene publication there were very few cases brought to trial in the United States between 1821–1870. Two publications dealing with birth control and sexual facts of life were prosecuted in Massachusetts[12] and Pennsylvania[13] respectively during this time period, but literary works like *Memoirs* were not subjected to extensive court litigation. Although Cleland's novel was published and distributed both in the United States and in England in these years, full-scale court cases against sellers did not occur. In England, people involved in the twenty-odd editions of *Memoirs* which were printed before 1845 were in many instances apprehended by authorities. However, they did not contest these legal actions; they paid fines and went briefly to jail.[14]

The first federal restriction on obscene items in the United States was contained in the Customs Law of 1842 which banned importation of indecent and obscene prints, paintings, etc. However, during the American Civil War (1861–1865) *Memoirs* was widely read in army camps. This evidence shows that in spite of federal restrictions *Memoirs* was being printed and distributed in the United States. Legal battles did not occur in America for the same reason as in England: offenders of the law went quietly to jail. Profits gained from publishing and selling books like *Memoirs* compensated for both the fines and short jail sentences imposed by judges.[15] Following the American Civil War Congress adopted a law declaring that the mailing of obscene publications was a criminal offense, although the post office was not given power to exclude such material from the mails. By 1873 the action of anti-vice groups under the leadership of Anthony Comstock of New York City succeeded in pushing Congress to pass the so-called Comstock Act. This statute became the federal standard for obscenity prosecutions in America.[16]

Anthony Comstock, in his capacity as a post office agent, was able to ban *Memoirs of a Woman of Pleasure*, among other publications. Comstock seized and confiscated sizable stocks of copies of *Memoirs* from the premises of publishers such as William Haynes who was reported to have made thousands of dollars from his sales of *Memoirs* alone, in spite of Comstock's best efforts. The legal and judicial actions of people like Comstock and members of the Congress who passed the Comstock Law were typical of the American approach to the problem of pornography at this time.[17]

ENGLISH PORNOGRAPHY STANDARDS: 1750s–1960s

The state and federal laws that developed in the United States in this period were affected by both parallel actions and historical precedents in England. During the late 1700s and early 1800s prosecutions of obscene libel were few in England. Although novels such as Fielding's *Tom Jones* and Sterne's *Tristram Shandy* contained large elements of questionable material, they were allowed to circulate freely. Authorities simply did not consider prosecuting obscene libel nearly so important as dealing with their political enemies. Although John Wilkes was prosecuted in 1763 for an obscene poem, it was widely assumed that the real motive was political and the case turned on technicalities rather than any definition of obscenity.[18] Two developments which at least indirectly affected future legal proceedings against pornography did take place during the late eighteenth century in England. First, the Libel Act of 1792 gave the English jury, rather than the judge, the right to decide the entire question of guilt or innocence in a libel case. Second, general search warrants which had allowed extensive police search for unspecified materials and publications were declared illegal. Authorities could no longer use this convenient warrant against printers and booksellers; judges were no longer the sole decision makers in defining obscenity.[19]

At the same time that law and practice moved in this direction, the publication of obscene books and pamphlets increased in England. Trade in cheap pornographic books and pictures became increasingly open and provoked growing opposition. The establishment of the militant Society for the Suppression of Vice in 1802 marked the opening of a new chapter in legal actions relating to obscenity. In the first five years of its existence, this English organization brought between thirty and forty prosecutions; it won convictions in every recorded case. By 1857 the Society had prosecuted 159 cases, securing convictions in all but five. The average sentence was around eight months. The published material judged obscene was seized and destroyed. English juries and judges were in agreement during the long period of the Napoleonic Wars. Fearing seditious libel that could undermine the nation during crisis, they made no attempt to distinguish between seditious and obscene libel. The greatest vigor in obscenity prosecution occurred during and immediately after the war, driving obscene materials underground. Yet by the 1850s pornographic works were actively circulating again and new ones were appearing on the open market. Old favorites like *Memoirs* were frequently republished, and a steady influx of foreign materials, mainly from France, resumed.[20]

Conflict between the increasingly stricter tastes of mid-Victorian England and this flow of pornography led to new efforts at control, this time by parliamentary legislation. In 1853 the Customs Consolidation Act specifically prohibited importation of "indecent or obscene prints, paintings, books, cards, lithographic or other engravings or any other indecent or obscene articles." An even more important measure was the Obscene Publications Act of 1857, known as Lord Campbell's Act. Lord Campbell, the Chief Justice of Queen's Bench, England's highest common law court, had become concerned over the nature and volume of the obscene book trade. The sale of such material was, according to Campbell, comparable to that of "poison more deadly than prussic acid, strychnine or arsenic."[21] It was to prohibit such danger that Campbell introduced his famous bill in Parliament and undertook the task of defining pornography. Exempting literary classics, Campbell focused on works "written for the single purpose of corrupting the morals of youth and of a nature calculated to shock the common feelings of decency in a well-regulated mind."[22] His bill did not create a new criminal offense or a new way to prosecute individuals: obscene libel had been defined as a misdemeanor recognizable under common law since *Rex v. Curll* in 1727. The main purpose of the act was to provide a way to seize the obscene/pornographic holdings of individuals and to dispose of them summarily. The act gave judges authority to issue warrants allowing police to search suspected premises; judges could also order the immediate destruction of books and prints whose publication could be considered "a misdemeanor proper to be prosecuted as such." Before passage the act was slightly modified to allow for an appeal before the material was actually destroyed.[23]

In the years following passage of Lord Campbell's Act, two important legal cases developed a standard test for obscenity and extended the scope of the 1857 act. The "Hicklin Rule" or test for obscenity resulted from an 1868 case involving one Henry Scott who was selling copies of a pamphlet published by a radical Protestant group and purporting to "unmask the depravity" of Catholic priests by detailing examples of their moral corruption. Scott, a religious fanatic, sold the pamphlets at cost with no profit for himself. When his pamphlets were ordered destroyed as obscene, he appealed the judge's decision to the court of quarter sessions. Benjamin Hicklin, the official in charge of such orders as recorder, decided to revoke the order on the grounds that the single purpose had not been to corrupt public morals but to expose problems within the Catholic Church. A further appeal was made by the authorities, bringing the case to the Court of Queen's Bench. Speaking for that court in the case of *Regina v. Hicklin*,[24] the Chief Justice overruled the recorder, Hicklin. Basing his decision on his own interpretation of Lord Campbell's Act, the Chief Justice announced what became known as the "Hicklin test" for obscenity. The central question was the "tendency of the matter . . . to deprave and corrupt those whose minds are open to such immoral influences and into whose hands a publication of this sort may fall."[25] The test, which allowed a publication to be banned if it had a "tendency to corrupt," constituted a "presumption of harm" standard.[26] It did not clearly identify, however, "those whose minds are open to such immoral influences." In both England and the United States judges either utilized the test or modified it in the years following its introduction. They emphasized "tendency" and considered three sorts of tendencies to be indictable: first, those which would arouse impure thoughts; second, those which would encourage impure actions; and third, those which would erode the prevailing standards of public morals. In most cases an offense against any one of the three, if proven, was sufficient for conviction.[27]

The second significant legal case which occurred following the passage of Lord Campbell's Act was *Regina v. Bradlaugh*.[28] This highly publicized trial focused on the printing of a sex manual advocating birth control and raised questions concerning the motives of publishers. In 1878 Charles Bradlaugh and Annie Besant were indicted for "unlawfully and wickedly devising and intending to vitiate and corrupt the morals of youth and of others" by publishing a "lewd, filthy, and obscene book" which constituted an obscene libel. The defense argued that the defendants had removed some controversial illustrations from their edition, and that their motives were to advocate a worthy cause, birth control.

The jury attempted to return a special verdict: the pamphlet itself was obscene since it was calculated to corrupt public morals, but the defendants were exonerated because they had no corrupt motives in publishing it. The court, however, ruled that intent was irrelevant and the judge threw out the jury's special verdict and entered a verdict of guilty. Upon further appeal the case was dismissed on a technicality. In the future the advocacy of birth control would be left safely outside the scope of obscene libel cases. However, the use of certain language or illustrations would not be defensible on grounds of good intentions of the publishers.[29]

As the nineteenth century drew toward its close, sporadic prosecutions of pornography continued. Although World War I and new generations of writers brought less consensus about pornography, prosecution continued. However, during World War II the number dropped. After the war, judicial reinterpretation of the standards of the Hicklin Rule brought existing law and judicial decision into conflict. Judges increasingly had trouble with the "most susceptible" persons criteria, "those whose minds are open to possible corruption." Earlier judicial opinions had utilized the standard of the innocent young girl and had equated "the mind of a fourteen year-old girl" with *Hicklin*'s "most susceptible" person.[30] Now judges began to refuse to do this. This struggle to give new definitions to judicial standards led to the first major change in English obscenity law in over a century. The Obscene Publications Act of 1959 officially modified both Lord Campbell's Act of 1857 and also the test from *Hicklin*. It provided that a publication should only be pronounced legally obscene if its effect "taken as a whole" was such as to "deprave and corrupt persons who are likely, having regard to all relevant circumstances to read, see, or hear it."[31] The law further allowed a defendant to produce expert witnesses and permitted a defense of the literary or social merits of the work. None of this had been allowed under the ruling in *Hicklin*.

In two early test cases involving the new law, however, it became evident that traditional standards and tests had not been abandoned. While *Lady Chatterly's Lover* was successfully defended under the Obscene Publications Act by an appeal to the "whole book concept" and to literary merit, in *Shaw v. DPP* (1961), 2 A.E.R.452, English courts reasserted the common law offense of "conspiring to corrupt public morals" and the powers of courts to "conserve the...moral welfare of the state." The concepts of *Rex v. Curll* were still very much alive, and the tradition of *Regina v. Hicklin* survived in spite of the 1959 act.

AMERICAN LEGAL AND JUDICIAL TESTS FOR PORNOGRAPHY: 1890s–1960s

American courts and judges had been quick to copy the standards that developed in England during the period from the 1750s to 1950s.

The test based on *Hicklin*, for example, came to be a touchstone for American jurists. Early in the 1890s the rule from *Regina v. Hicklin* was applied in the United States in two cases: *In re Arentsen*[32] and *In re Worthington Co.*[33] The latter case identified the susceptible individual of *Hicklin* as the "common man." The social and economic status of purchasers and readers became an important factor in determining obscenity according to the New York judge who heard the case. His elaboration of the *Hicklin* test focused on the need to keep obscene books from being bought "by the class of people from whom unclean publications ought to be withheld." Thus the *Hicklin* precedent was extended to include not only the juvenile but also lower social and economic classes of individuals.

One part of the English standard of *Regina v. Hicklin* was challenged by American judges. Although some U.S. courts followed the English practice of judging obscenity by the effect of *isolated* passages on the most susceptible persons, other courts decided to consider the context of a work rather than the isolated passage. For example, the "whole book" concept was applied in two New York cases in the early 1900s. *St. Hubert Guild v. Quinn*[34] tested the extent to which passages considered obscene dominated a publication using the stated formula, "the *pervasiveness* of patently offensive materials." *Halsey v. New York Society for the Suppression of Vice*[35] also applied *Hicklin*, but moved from isolated passages to the whole book concept.

One especially notable case to utilize the English standard of *Regina v. Hicklin* was *U.S. v. Kennerly*.[36] Here Judge Learned Hand indicated that he was unhappy with the *Hicklin* test, but that he felt bound by it and by precedent established in its wake. However, he wanted to move beyond a test that seemed to limit adult reading to what was safe for children. As a result Judge Hand created a corollary to *Hicklin* which added "community standards" as a criterion in determining obscenity.

With an English standard like *Regina v. Hicklin* exerting such influence in American obscenity cases it is not surprising that *Memoirs of a Woman of Pleasure*, obscene in England, would likewise remain an underground publication in America. However, American legal proceedings in which *Memoirs* figured following the first 1821 case did not lead to full dress court battles with judicial decisions. The experience of two New York City booksellers in the post–World War I period demonstrated this. In 1923 two New York booksellers, Maurice Inmon and Max Gottschalk, were arrested for selling *Memoirs*. They had unwittingly sold the book to an agent of the Vice Society. Legal proceedings were uncomplicated and simple. On December 12, 1923, the city magistrate "ordered them held on $1,000.00 bail each until tried in the Court of Special Session." When the case came to trial in March 1924 both booksellers pleaded guilty of violating Section 1141 of the New York State Penal Law. The judges read *Memoirs*, pronounced it obscene, and booksellers Inmon and Gottschalk did not claim that there were any constitutional protections broad enough to cover *Memoirs*. The three-judge court imposed a fine of $250 each as an alternative to thirty days in jail. Even *Publisher's Weekly*, a major trade journal, refused to criticize the court findings, commenting instead that the suppression of "such admittedly obscene books is a salutary measure of which the booktrade may well approve." It was not until the early 1930s that the editors of *Publisher's Weekly* would begin to question whether "such a nebulous concept of obscenity . . . could ever provide a sufficient basis for proceedings at law." And it would still be almost thirty years before American printers, publishers, and book sellers would demand constitutional protection for *Memoirs*.[37]

In the meantime U.S. court proceedings continued to depend on *Regina v. Hicklin* in the judiciary's search for legal standards and criteria. While applying the English rule, American judicial opinions continued to elaborate and refine this standard. American judges raised questions about the lessons authors were trying to teach in their books and attempted to balance obscene sections against the central theme in order to determine author's intent. Some judges also implied that obscene passages would be tolerated if, and only if, the literary work actually sought to improve human conditions or to teach a moral or social lesson. Other judges focused on the effect of the book on the average reader, seeking to establish linkage between anti-social action and the reading of obscene books. Attempts were also made to link criminal behavior to the reading of pornographic literature and to rule against publication on that basis. Many judges discussed the idea of using literary merit established through expert testimony to escape the straightjacket of *Hicklin*'s standard. However, courts could not agree on this any more than they could agree concerning language and style as a defense against the charge of obscenity. Some judges seemed willing to accept the original argument advanced by John Cleland in his own defense, namely, that the use of a clever, polished style devoid of impure words was sufficient to absolve a publication of obscenity charges. Other judges, however, saw an even greater danger in a "felicitous" style using "exquisite settings" and "perfumed words."[38]

The struggles of American judges with the test of *Regina v. Hicklin* reached a high point during the 1930s in the case of *United States v. One Book Entitled "Ulysses."*[39] Two central approaches of *Hicklin* had long created dissatisfaction: the use of isolated passages to judge obscenity and the use of the "most susceptible person" as the barometer for determining "material that might corrupt." In *Ulysses* American judges, including the renowned Learned Hand and his cousin Augustus Hand, as well as others, modified the English definition of the audience by creating the average man standard. This new definition provided for a more sophisticated audience than that originally defined in *Regina v. Hicklin*. In addition, U.S. courts shifted away from the isolated passage approach of *Hicklin*. They added tests focusing on the intent of the author—no "dirt for dirt's sake"—and on the opinion of literary critics. This approach moved American courts toward a "whole book" standard for obscenity prosecutions.

Attempts to move beyond *Hicklin* were also demonstrated in the 1949 decision of *Commonwealth v. Gordon*[40] in which the trial judge raised an entirely different question and test, namely, "Can freedom of speech and press be limited if there is no evidence that a book has created a 'clear and present' danger to society?" Although the judge thought that this was an unprecedented approach in determining obscenity, in actuality he was evoking an English precedent even older than *Regina v. Hicklin*. The "clear and present danger" test of *Commonwealth v. Gordon* focused on the creation of a breach of the peace action with obscenity linked to specific dangerous or violent actions. This idea was not new to English precedent; it had been at the heart of Sir Charles Sedley's case in 1663. London courts in this case had defined obscene words and behavior as those tending to create a disturbance or breach of the king's peace which courts could punish. The obscene gestures of Sir Charles had, even without actual physical violence, constituted a breach of the peace—a clear and present danger. Sedley's appearance and actions created a form of clear and present danger in that offended bystanders could have easily rioted. Morover, due to the fact that seditious and obscene libel had often been linked in English practice, as in *Curll*, the clear and present danger standard was a well-established English test long before the American one in *Commonwealth v. Gordon*.

It was the constitutional focus on freedom of speech and press therefore, rather than the clear and present danger aspect, which became the unique contribution of American judges in the search for standards governing obscenity prosecution. By 1957 in the case of *Butler v. Michigan*,[41] U.S. Supreme Court Justice Felix Frankfurter used the freedom of speech constitutional argument to stop Michigan from implementing a state statute which, under state judicial interpretation, defined obscenity as "tending to the corruption of the morals of youth." This state statute as interpreted embodied the tests and standard of *Regina v. Hicklin* which, according to the U.S. Supreme Court, curtailed "one of those liberties [freedom of speech] of the individual now enshrined in the Due Process Clause of the Fourteenth Amendment." This new focus on constitutionally protected rights, however, did not mean that the standards and tests of *Regina v. Hicklin* were abandoned. In fact the 1957 landmark case of *Roth v. United States*[42] carried both traditions forward. According to the U.S. Supreme Court at that time, obscenity was "not within the area of constitutionally protected speech or press." Obscenity, the majority ruled, was to be judged by its tendency to arouse sexual thoughts. This part of the Court's ruling therefore retained an essential feature of *Regina v. Hicklin*: the "bad tendency doctrine" prohibiting any expression with a tendency to have a detrimental effect. Actual harm need not occur. In addition, however, a second part of the Court's opinion in *Roth* held that ideas "having even the slightest redeeming social importance" had the full protection of guarantees of the Bill of Rights. The Court also continued to apply the American standards and tests which had modified the Hicklin test to read "whether to the *average* [as opposed to the "most susceptible"] person, applying contemporary community standards, the dominant theme of the material taken *as a whole* [as opposed to an isolated passage] appeals to prurient interest." This was the prevailing judicial criteria for judging obscenity in the United States in the early 1960s when the history of literary obscenity cases came full circle with new English and American legal actions against John Cleland's *Memoirs of a Woman of Pleasure*.

A PORNOGRAPHIC CLASSIC RETURNS TO CENTER STAGE IN MODERN ENGLISH COURTS: ACT TWO

While Americans had struggled to modify the *Regina v. Hicklin* standards for obscenity, English practice had continued to apply it along with other traditional precedents. In general, books like *Memoirs* had not been involved in landmark legal cases in England during the 1800s and early 1900s. After 1749 *Memoirs* appeared only clandestinely in England. English common law did not function in this period to close down dealers and booksellers totally. Only the books named in the warrant were confiscated and the profits earned by distributors were usually enough to compensate for this loss. *Memoirs* thus never disappeared completely from the public scene in England, although its sale was always under the counter and often at inflated prices. The 1960s, however, brought *Memoirs* again into the spotlight in England as well as in the United States.[43]

An English publishing company, Mayflower Books, scheduled a soft cover, unexpurgated *Fanny Hill: Memoirs of a Woman of Pleasure*, for publication in November 1963. Mayflower had observed that in the United States G. P. Putnam's Sons had published *Memoirs* and won a significant—although not final—court battle in New York State during this time period. Mayflower expected some English legal action against their publication but they were not prepared for the events that followed. Official English action against *Memoirs* began at a small London shop in Tottenham Court Road. Owned by Gold and Sons, The Magic Shop sold cheap books and magic tricks. It apparently catered to juveniles. The shop and its owners did not have a good reputation and this fact would be of legal significance. The English court authorities also took note of the fact that Mayflower Books, Ltd. did not have a truly high institutional standing and did not retail exclusively through bona fide bookstores and outlets. The Magic Shop where *Memoirs* was openly distributed and sold at this time was run by men described as shady entrepreneurs who were often in trouble with the law. They had engaged in illegal sales of books before and were involved in the emerging pornographically illustrated magazine trade. The Magic Shop itself was not a true bookstore and was regarded as a seedy establishment.[44]

A provocative window advertisement in The Magic Shop during the first week of November 1963 had alerted police to the fact that *Memoirs* was appearing openly and that it was being billed as Banned in America—a claim designed to excite interest of passers-by. A police inspector at the instigation of the director of Public Prosecutions called on the shop's manager who asserted that *Memoirs* was legitimate since he was not selling it to juveniles. The police, however, sought a warrant from the chief metropolitan magistrate at the Bow Street Magistrate's Court. Sir Robert Blundell, who held the position at that time, read the book and immediately issued the search warrant. The police descended upon the shop and confiscated 171 paperback copies of *Memoirs*. The shop's owner, Ralph Gold, was served with a summons ordering him to appear in Magistrate's Court and to show cause why the books should not be forfeited. He was charged under the 1959 Obscene Publications Act, Section 3, and trial was set for February 1964. Mayflower Books, Ltd. had already distributed some 82,000 copies of *Memoirs*; however, the firm immediately ceased distribution.[45]

Mayflower Books, Ltd. had assumed that they would be the defendants in the case and would be allowed to counter the charge of obscenity in *Memoirs* with the defense of literary merit and social value. Their attorney wrote to the director of Public Prosecutions urging the government to proceed against the company rather than one bookseller. He pointed out that this was permitted under one section of the 1959 Obscene Publications Act; he also urged a jury trial. However, the director of Public Prosecution decided to use a different section of the obscene Publications Act, and this legal strategy placed Mayflower Books, Ltd. at a disadvantage. It meant simply that the disreputable owners of The Magic Shop would be the primary target: Mayflower Books Publishing Company could only join in the suit. In addition the trial would be held before a single judge and not before a jury. The judge could thus act under his summary jurisdiction power. These legal proceedings allowed the prosecution to highlight the issue of distribution by the publisher and to emphasize the nature of average readers (juveniles) attracted to the book as it was being sold in the shop on Tottenham Court Road.[46]

With Mayflower Books, Ltd. consigned to this role while footing all legal bills, the case against the Golds for selling and distributing *Memoirs* came up for argument on January 20, 1964. The prosecution's legal strategy was to establish that the book, taken as a whole, was obscene, would corrupt the average reader, and had no redeeming historical, literary, or social value. There were seven major points of dispute which would be raised during the trial: the intent of the author; the intent of publisher and distributor; the question of "a morbid, sick, or degrading [prurient]"[47] treatment of sex; the relationship of the book to currently acceptable community standards in publication; [48] the effect of the book on "persons . . . likely, having regard to all circumstances, to read it";[49] the question of historical, social, and literary value found in the publication; and finally, the nature of the book as a whole.[50]

Among these points of dispute which defense and prosecution argued, the issue of publisher's intent was more significant than that of author's intent. Both sides apparently agreed that Cleland's objective in 1748 had been to make money. In America attorneys would hedge on the point, emphasizing the difficulty of assessing Cleland's mind after the passage of 200 years. However, in England defense and prosecution did not dispute author's intent and the intent of the publisher and the distributor became the central focus. The defense stressed the former and the prosecution the latter. The prosecution in particular emphasized the pandering motive of the distributors (the Golds) by describing their advertisements and the total environment of the shop. The defense countered with the argument that the publishers had deliberately chosen a book jacket for *Memoirs* that was unobtrusive, "dignified and unlurid."[51]

The question of prurient interest was also much debated, with the defense arguing that the publication did not present a morbid, sick, or degrading treatment of sex. The defense relied on expert witnesses, primarily writers and literary critics, in an attempt to document the normal and happy portrayal of the sex relationship. The prosecution, on the other hand, focused on scenes from *Memoirs* that dealt with perversion and abnormal sex practices.

The fourth issue concerned the question of the book's relationship to contemporary community standards, and whether it went beyond current novels in its explicit descriptions. Both sides argued the question, "Does the book, taken as a whole, have the effect of depraving and corrupting persons who, having regard to all relevant circumstances, read it?"[52] The prosecution argued that *Memoirs*' appeal was almost totally to a sex-oriented audience and not to a literary one. In addition, The Magic Shop was known to cater to young people wanting to buy jokes, games, and tricks. Would the average person who came into contact with *Memoirs* be depraved and corrupted by it? The prosecution insisted that the cheap price [3s2d or $0.50] made it available to everyone and that no one would read *Memoirs* except for the sexual titillation which it provided. People interested in literature would not patronize The Magic Shop and the average person who would buy a book there would not likely be interested in history. The defense insisted that *Memoirs* contained nothing "which is not to be found in other books" and asked the court not to speculate on the motives of the purchasers in buying the books.[53] The legal debate concluded with the question: "Is there any social, literary, or historical value to be found in the book?" The defense pointed out specific scenes that dealt with issues of eighteenth-century life; the prosecution emphasized the scarcity of such redeeming material.

The verdict of Sir Robert Blundell was that the 171 copies of *Memoirs* which had been seized by the police should be forfeited and destroyed. The judge in typical English fashion did not retire to consider his verdict, delivering it immediately after the defense concluded. First, he noted that the social value argument as presented by the expert witnesses was "unconvincing." Second, evaluating all the other points raised by the defense—from publisher's intent through contemporary community standards—the judge concluded that the defenders of *Memoirs* "had not established their case on the balance of probabilities."[54]

The decision was not appealed by Mayflower Books for several reasons. The company had argued from the beginning that the proceeding had created an extreme hardship for them as publishers. Mayflower Books had actively sought to appear as defendants and not as third parties to the case. An appeal from the adverse decision of Sir Robert Blundell would require a complete re-hearing, starting all over again before the London quarter sessions. Even if the case should be won there, it still would not establish a precedent for all of England. To defend *Memoirs*, Mayflower Books would have had to support every distributor of their publications from one end of the country to the other—wherever local police decided to move against it. None of the decisions would be final in the sense of a U.S. Supreme Court ruling, or as it might have been if the book had been charged (rather than the distributors) and the publishers cited as defendants. Hence, Mayflower Books, Ltd. decided not to appeal: it was all too expensive. It was not the right case, at the right time, in the right place, with the right parties.

A second reason was actually part of the first. The period after the *Memoirs* trial was marked by numerous police raids on booksellers, especially in northern England. In February and March 1964, the Manchester police raided city bookshops and seized all editions of *Memoirs*. The C. Nicholls and Co.'s 4,000 copies were impounded, and the firm was summoned to court. In April, the Manchester court found *Memoirs* obscene and the Nicholls's stock was ordered to be "forfeit and destroyed." Similar actions occurred in Birmingham, Brighton, and Sheffield. The multiplicity of these actions confirmed Mayflower Books' worst fears about the mounting court costs necessary to defend *Memoirs* due to the number of proceedings and the lack of finality of any single local court ruling. Public opinion in England was also divided at this time, and Mayflower Books was not sure of winning even with a jury trial. Debates over the Bow Street decision had rocked the press and had led to intense debaters in Parliament, with neither side able to win a clear victory for its position. This state of public confusion convinced Mayflower Books that the sensible, financially expedient course of action was to produce an expurgated version which might be acceptable. This was done, and the original, unexpurgated text did not reappear until 1970. Technically, therefore, the unexpurgated *Memoirs* remained a banned book in England although no longer prosecuted.[55]

THE PRIMA BALLERINA OF PORNOGRAPHY RETURNS TO AMERICAN COURTS

Meanwhile in the United States the series of legal battles involving *Memoirs* continued. These had started again in 1963 when G. P. Putnam's Sons published the former "prima ballerina" of pornography; the book's reputation made legal action inevitable.[56] Action against *Memoirs* could have been brought by the federal government or by the various state governments. Putnam's preferred a federal prosecution: they faced instead three state actions. Nevertheless, unlike Mayflower Books, Putnam's could hope for the finality of a U.S. Supreme Court ruling even though the cases worked their way up through state courts. In each state—New York, New Jersey, and Massachusetts—different local laws allowed slightly different proceedings, and the outcome also differed. Ultimately only the case from Massachusetts would be argued before and decided by the U.S. Supreme Court. A final ruling on the legal status of *Memoirs* would result from this case proceeding. However, the actions that accompanied all of the legal proceedings in each of the three states would be relevant for a final disposition of the issue by the Supreme Court. Judges do influence Supreme Court justices, and issues and arguments raised in one court will often appear in another.

Legal proceedings against *Memoirs* in New York began when the district attorneys of the five boroughs along with the New York City police commissioner went to court to secure an order directed at Putnam's to show cause why all copies of *Memoirs* should not be seized and confiscated. *Memoirs* won its first major victory in the hearing that followed. This was short-lived however, for on appeal the New York Appellate Division ruled against the book. Putnam's then carried their appeal to the highest state court of New York, the court of appeals, where *Memoirs* won a victory again in *Larkin v. Putnam's Sons*.[57]

In Massachusetts, meanwhile, the state attorney general started action to have *Memoirs* banned. The first trial resulted in a ruling against the book, and was maintained on appeal by a four to three ruling in *Attorney General v. A Book Named "John Cleland's Memoirs of a Woman of Pleasure."*[58] In New Jersey an investigation by the county prosecutor's office prompted Putnam's to seek a declaratory judgement in *G. P. Putnam's Sons v. Calissi;*[59] this was a legal effort to avoid a possible criminal prosecution by the state. The state's response was to seek an injunction to ban the distribution of *Memoirs* in New Jersey. This case produced another anti-*Memoirs* decision. Putnam's did not pursue the New Jersey case any further since the issue was already pending in Massachusetts's highest court. All of these legal actions had resulted in a number of close, split decisions. Nevertheless, the final score card seemed to indicate that *Memoirs* had lost more actions than it had won. The variety of issues raised in all of these state proceedings demonstrated the complexity of the pornography question; they would remain in dispute throughout the federal court proceeding.

The issues that surfaced in all of the state proceedings were remarkably similar to those argued before Sir Robert Blundell in the Bow Street Magistrate's Court, London. In fact an analysis reveals clearly that there were seven major issues which appeared with regularity in all of the proceedings: (1) the author's intent; (2) the intent of the publisher; (3) a dominant appeal to prurient interest in sex;[60] (4) a patent offensiveness to community standards;[61] (5) the impact on the average person; (6) the utter lack of social value; and (7) the nature of the book as a whole.

In the New York proceedings the judge who granted the preliminary injunction against *Memoirs* focused on the issue of whether the book was "patently offensive and without social value." He assessed its "impact on the average person in the community" and found that it appealed to "a prurient interest . . . in sex." The judges in the Appellate Division in New York considered social value and community standards. How did *Memoirs* compare with currently accepted literature in terms of its "shocking" nature? They asked questions concerning Cleland's intent in writing; the reputation of G. P. Putnam's Sons as a publishing house; Putnam's motive in publishing *Memoirs*; and the dominant purpose of the entire book. The Massachusetts courts focused on the question of social value and on the applicability of tests for prurient appeal and patent offensiveness. These judges paid special attention to the dominant nature of the book; to its comparison with contemporary novels; to the effect of the book on the average reader; and to the question of literary or social value. They also questioned the publication and distribution of *Memoirs* with specific attention being paid to the motive and intent of the publisher. In New Jersey the questions and focus repeated these familiar tests.[62]

Memoirs before the U.S. Supreme Court

By the time the case came before the U.S. Supreme Court in 1966, the terminology had become settled and the framework for legal argument was fixed. The case was argued before a court composed of Chief Justice Earl Warren and Justices Brennan, Black, Douglas, Clark, Harlan, Stewart, White, and Fortas. These justices created in their decision a threefold test for obscenity which contained most of the phrases and concepts that had dominated the judicial proceedings both in the state courts below and in earlier English cases. For a work to be judged obscene the following three factors had to be present: the "dominant theme of the material, taken as a whole," had to be shown to appeal to a "prurient interest in sex"; the material had to be "patently offensive" and an affront to "contemporary community standards relating to... sexual matters"; and the material had to be "utterly without redeeming social value."[63]

Three of the justices also held that the intent of the publisher, the circumstances of the production, sale, and publicity, could be relevant in determining whether a publication was protected by the federal constitution. Commercial exploitation for the sale of prurient appeal, to the exclusion of all other values, might justify the conclusion that the book was utterly without redeeming social importance. Two justices focused on an issue that had not been debated in the state courts, namely, the First Amendment guarantee of freedom of speech. Justices Black and Douglas regarded this as an absolute ban on governmental suppression. Justice Clark, in dissent, stressed an additional test. He looked for the intent of author and that of the publisher. Clark held that books which were commercially exploited to attract readers through a morbid appeal to sex could be banned as obscene. In addition, authors who designed a book solely to "prey upon prurient and carnal proclivities for pecuniary advantage" could have their works be deemed obscene and hence banned.

Attorneys in their oral arguments and briefs before the U.S. Supreme Court had raised and debated a number of English case precedents and themes dating back to the 1700s. The justices pursued these questions for two reasons. First, they were interested in finding out if the author of *Memoirs* had been involved in legal actions. Second, they wanted information on obscenity prosecution in the early 1700s in England. In order to satisfy the Court upon these points, counsel responded to questions and submitted additional briefs. Counsel for *Memoirs*, Mr. Charles Rembar, answered the questions concerning legal action in 1749–1750 against John Cleland. He based his reply on the best-known research of the 1960s which suggested that, "the author himself was not prosecuted."[64] More recent scholarship, however, indicates that Cleland *was* subjected to several legal actions.[65] It was this line of questioning that led Justice William O. Douglas to devote two and one-half pages of his opinion to the English history of legal prosecutions of obscenity and to the case precedents of *Read* and *Curll*.

Justice Clark focused on testimony relating to Cleland's intent in writing *Memoirs* and for evidence of a pandering intent on the part of the publisher, G. P. Putnam's and Sons.[66] Analysis of the historical and literary views about *Memoirs*' value led Clark to conclude that Cleland's intent had been solely to appeal to a morbid interest in sex for the purpose of personal, financial gain. The Introduction to Putnam's edition of *Memoirs*, along with the book jacket covers and advertisements convinced Justice Clark that the publishing house had indeed engaged in pandering and should be penalized.[67]

Oral argument before the Court included a debate over the historic English precedent, *Rex v. Curll*. An *amicus curia* brief filed by "Citizens for Decent Literature" had made extensive use of *Curll*. The definition of obscenity in *Curll* was used to condemn *Memoirs*. Defense counsel, Charles Rembar, spent one-sixth of his total time for argument in debating this interpretation. In addition, he filed a "Supplemental Reply Brief" to answer in still greater detail the arguments about *Curll* raised in the Citizens for Decent Literature's brief. The attorney drew the Court's attention to a different point in this historic English case: seditious libel had been linked to Curll's obscenity charge. Rembar argued that Edmund Curll was prosecuted more for publishing government secrets than for pornography. This fact, not previously noted by the U.S. courts, raised doubts and fears about letting government loose with powers to prosecute obscenity easily: It could become a cover for silencing political criticism.[68]

In their final analysis the U.S. Supreme Court refused to find *Memoirs* obscene. The vote was six to three, but the justices wrote seven opinions. Each of the three dissenting justices—Clark, Harlan, and White—wrote a separate dissent. The majority was divided into three groups. Justice Brennan wrote an opinion which was joined by Justice Fortas and Chief Justice Earl Warren. Justice Douglas wrote a separate concurrence. Justices Black and Stewart concurred in the judgment but focused on different arguments and legal reasoning. The problems in defining pornography/obscenity and in articulating standards for governmental control could scarcely be considered as resolved by such a fragmented decision.

PORNOGRAPHY IN TODAY'S COURTS

In the years that followed the *Memoirs* decision, the difficulties inherent in that case's judicial test became obvious. The struggle to apply the

Memoirs test produced a sense of futility and unease among the justices themselves. Each justice tended to focus on a slightly different element of the test, thus creating several separate tests. This divergence of opinion soon demonstrated that the Supreme Court would be unable to offer clear guidelines to legislatures or to other courts, and confusion increased.

The stage was thus set for other modifications of the definition of and tests for pornography. A 1973 group of five[69] cases offered the opportunity for the Court to redefine standards. Chief Justice Warren E. Burger, speaking for a majority of five justices, drew back from the *Memoirs* test for obscenity: "utterly without redeeming social value." He noted that "the *Memoirs* test has been abandoned as unworkable by its author [Justice William Brennan] and no member of the Court today supports the *Memoirs* formulation." The Supreme Court in *Miller v. California*[70] then returned to a test that was very close to *Regina v. Hicklin*. The new three-pronged test, in the language of Chief Justice Burger, read as follows:

The basic guidelines for the trier of fact must be: (a) whether "the *average* person, applying contemporary community standards" would find that the work, *taken as a whole*, appeals to the prurient interest [ROTH], (b) whether the work depicts or describes, in a patently offensive way, sexual conduct specifically defined by the applicable state law, and (c) whether the work, taken as a whole, lacks serious literary, artistic, political, or scientific value.

Some of the justices, however, saw this test as only a "restatement of the *Roth-Memoirs* definition of obscenity."[71] The first part of the *Miller* test was based on *Roth* and actually was a modification of the familiar English precedent, *Regina v. Hicklin*. Chief Justice Burger's Miller opinion in 1973 echoed one of Lord Chief Justice Campbell's in 1857 as each reacted to the pornographic trade of his time period. Lord Campbell, arguing for England's first major obscenity law, called pornography a "poison more deadly than prussic acid, strychnine, or arsenic." In like manner, Chief Justice Burger, asserting in *Miller* the need for censorship of pornography, declared, "Civilized people do not allow unregulated access to heroin because it is a derivative of medicinal morphine." For both men, obscenity was comparable to drugs which ultimately poisoned and destroyed their users.

During the 1980s the U.S. Supreme Court in several cases attempted to explain their latest test. In *Brockett v. Spokane Arcades, Inc.*, 472 U.S.491 (1985) the word "prurient" was defined as sexual responses over and beyond those "characterized as normal." Two years later the Supreme Court affirmed the responsibility of juries to apply the test of "contemporary community standards" in order to assess the patent offensiveness of the work and its appeal to prurient interests. However, juries were not authorized to determine literary, artistic, political, or scientific value. Instead, the "reasonable man" standard which had modified *Hicklin's* "most susceptible person" test was resurrected by the Supreme Court as a guiding principle[72] to determine the value of a publication. Justice White's opinion for the Court noted that unlike prurient appeal and patent offensiveness, "literary, artistic, political, or scientific value ... is not [determined] by contemporary community standards.... The proper inquiry is ... whether a *reasonable person* would find such value in the material, taken as a whole." And in 1989 in *Sable v. F.C.C.*[73] the U.S. Supreme Court, while upholding federal bans on obscene interstate commercial telephone messages, denied governmental power to ban indecent communications based solely on the "corrupting the minds and morals of youth" concept. Writing for the majority, Justice White declared that one section of the federal law dealing with indecent communications had the "invalid effect of limiting the content of adult telephone conversations to that which is suitable for children to hear." The context of *Sable* was new; the standards and questions which were debated were old.

And so the debate continues. The long-standing problem of obscenity/pornography continues to exist on both sides of the Atlantic. The tests and standards from earliest English cases have continually permeated the opinions of American courts. Citations of English precedents, arguments based on English history, and references to English cases have long been standard practice for American judges on state court benches, on lower federal courts, and on the U.S. Supreme Court. Sometimes the judges have adhered to English standards precisely; at other times they have modified them; again and again they have returned to debate them anew.

NOTES

1. Commonwealth v. Peter Holmes, 17 Mass. 335 (1821).

2. Ralph Straus, *The Unspeakable Curll: Being Some Account of Edmund Curll, Bookseller, to Which is Added a Full List of His Books* (London: Chapman and Hall, 1927), pp. 99–104.

3. Regina v. Read (1708), 11 Mod. Rep. 142.

4. Rex v. Curll (1727), 17 St. Tr. 153.

5. Laurence Hanson, *Government and the Press, 1695–1763* (Oxford: Clarendon Press, 1936; reprint 1967), pp. 46–47.

6. William H. Epstein, *John Cleland: Images of a Life* (New York: Columbia University Press, 1974), pp. 4–6; 61–64; 71–80.

7. Ibid., pp. 79–80.

8. R.W.G. Vail, "A Curtain Call for Benjamin Gomez," *The Colophon*, Part 9 (1932).

9. Ralph Thompson, "Deathless Lady," *The Colophon*, New Series vol. 1, no. 2 (1935), pp. 207–20.

10. Commonwealth v. Stillman Howe, WSJC, 4–20 (April 1820) and Commonwealth v. Peter Holmes, 17 Mass. 335 (1821).

11. Sedley was an integral member of the court of King Charles of England. He is described as "one of the lewdest writers" of Restoration comedies and bawdy poems. See Leo M. Alpert, "Judicial Censorship of Obscene Literature," 52 *Harvard Law Review* (1938), pp. 40–43.

12. Charles Knowlton in 1832 was fined and imprisoned in Massachusetts for writing *The Fruits of Philosophy*, a contraceptive manual. In England Charles Bradlaugh and Annie Besant published the manual and set in motion a series of legal actions. See David Tribe, *Questions of Censorship* (New York: St. Martin's Press, 1973), p. 25.

13. The book was entitled *Secrets of Generation*. The Pennsylvania case was Commonwealth v. Landis, 8 Philadelphia 453 (1870).

14. David Loth, *The Erotic in Literature* (London: Secker and Warburg, 1961), pp. 89–99, 108.

15. Thompson, "Deathless Lady," pp. 219–20.

16. Paul S. Boyer, *Purity in Print: The Vice Society Movement and Book Censorship in America* (New York: Charles Scribner's Sons, 1968), p. 183.

17. Ibid.

18. Frederick S. Siebert, *Freedom of the Press in England, 1476–1776: The Rise and Decline of Government Control* (Urbana: University of Illinois Press, 1965), pp. 42–49, 243–61, 376–79.

19. Norman St. John-Stevas, *Obscenity and the Law* (London: Secker and Warburg, 1956), pp. 145–46.

20. Ibid., pp. 38–67.

21. 146 Hansard Parliamentary Debates (3d ser.) 327 (1857), cited by St. John-Stevas, *Obscenity and the Law*, p. 67.

22. Ibid.

23. Ibid., p. 66.

24. Regina v. Hicklin (1868), L.R.3Q.B.360.

25. Ibid.

26. Glenn A. Phelps and Robert A. Poirier, eds., *Contemporary Debates on Civil Liberties: Enduring Constitutional Questions* (Lexington, MA: D. C. Heath and Co., 1985), pp. 51–68.

27. St. John-Stevas, *Obscenity and the Law*, pp. 126–27.

28. Regina v. Bradlaugh (1877), 2Q.B.D. 569.

29. Ibid.

30. St. John-Stevas, *Obscenity and the Law*, pp. 112–16. See also E.C.S. Wade and G. Godfrey Phillips, *Constitutional and Administrative Law*, 9th ed. (New York: Longman, 1977), pp. 478–79.

31. Wade and Phillips, *Constitutional and Administrative Law*, pp. 479–83.

32. In re Arentsen, 26 W.N.C.359 (Q.S. Ct. Phil., 1890).

33. In re Worthington Co., 30 N.Y.S. 361 (1894).

34. St. Hubert Guild v. Quinn, 118 N.Y.S. 582 (Sup. Ct. 1909).

35. Halsey v. New York Society for the Suppression of Vice, 234 N.Y.1 (1922).

36. U.S. v. Kennerley, 209 F. 119 (S.D.N.Y.) 1913.

37. "Two Booksellers Arrested on Sumner Complaint," *Publisher's Weekly*, Dec, 22, 1923, p. 1938. See also "Gottschalk Fined for Obscene Book Sale," *Publisher's Weekly*, March 8, 1924, p. 834.

38. Felice F. Lewis, *Literature, Obscenity and Law* (Carbondale and Edwardsville: Southern Illinois University Press, 1976), pp. 1–24, 42. Read "felicitous" as "happy."

39. U.S. v. One Book Entitled "Ulysses," 72 F. 2d 705 (1934).

40. Commonwealth v. Gordon, 66 Pa. D. and C. 101 (1949).

41. Butler v. Michigan, 352 U.S. 380 (1957).

42. Roth v. United States, 354 U.S. 476 (1957).

43. *The Times* (London), January 21, 1964, p. 7.

44. John Sutherland, *Offensive Literature: Decensorship in Britain 1960–1982* (Totowa, N.J.: Barnes and Noble Books, 1982), p. 32.

45. H. Montgomery Hyde, *A History of Pornography* (London: Heinemann, 1964), p. 209. See also *The Times* (London), January 28, 1964, p. 7.

46. Ibid., p. 210.

47. Ibid., pp. 211–14.

48. Ibid., pp. 224–25; 233.

49. Ibid., pp. 210, 212, 216, 219–23.

50. Ibid., p. 229.

51. *The Times* (London), January 21, 1964, p. 7.

52. *The Times* (London), January 28, 1964, p. 7 and February 11, 1964, p. 6.

53. Hyde, *Pornography*, pp. 111, 210, 216, 222, 223.

54. Sutherland, *Offensive Literature*, pp. 32, 38.

55. Ibid.

56. Charles Rembar, *The End of Obscenity: The Trials of Lady Chatterly, Tropic of Cancer, and Fanny Hill* (New York: Random House, 1968), pp. 224, 459, 460.

57. Larkin v. G. P. Putnam's Sons, 14 N.Y.S. 2d 399 (1964). See Rembar, *The End of Obscenity*, pp. 224–25.

58. Attorney General of Massachusetts v. A Book Named "John Cleland's Memoirs of a Woman of Pleasure," 349 Mass. 69 (1965).

59. G. P. Putnam's Sons v. Calissi, 86 N.J. Super. 82 (1964).

60. "Prurient" interest is usually defined as a restless sexual craving which is accompanied by thoughts and desires which are lascivious (lewd, lustful).

61. "Patently" offensive indicates that the material is *clearly* and *obviously* against public standards and values.

62. Rembar, *The End of Obscenity*, pp. 236–335.

63. A Book Named "John Cleland's Memoirs of a Woman of Pleasure" v. Attorney General of Massachusetts, 383 U.S. 413 (1966).

64. Rembar, *The End of Obscenity*, pp. 459–61; 469–73.

65. See Epstein, *John Cleland*, pp. 4, 75, 80, 82.

66. "Pandering" refers to an exploitation of and catering to weakness of others.

67. A Book Named "John Cleland's Memoirs of a Woman of Pleasure v. Attorney General of Massachusetts, 383 U.S. 413 (1966). See especially p. 441–45.

68. Rembar, *The End of Obscenity*, pp. 459–61; 469–73.

69. Miller v. California, 413 U.S. 15 (1973). Paris Adult Theater I v. Slaton,

413 U.S. 49 (1973). Kaplan v. California, 413 U.S. 115 (1973). United States v. 12 200 ft. Reels of Super 8mm, 413 U.S. 123 (1973). United States v. Orito, 413 U.S. 139 (1973).

  70. Miller v. California, 413 U.S. 15 (1973).
  71. Paris Adult Theatre I v. Slaton, 413 U.S. 49 (1973).
  72. Pope v. Illinois, 481 U.S. 497 (1987).
  73. Sable v. F.C.C., 492 U.S. 115 (1989).

Chapter 4

The Criminal Insanity Defense: English and American Attorneys

Society has struggled for many centuries to find a proper balance between the political need to defend the established order and the moral imperative to protect the mentally disabled, even when they commit criminal acts. This struggle has taken place more in courtrooms than in legislative chambers, for legislators have preferred to leave definition of mental incapacity and disposition of criminal cases involving insanity pleas to the courts. Legal case studies of insanity pleas remain, therefore, essential to any understanding of the meaning of "not guilty by reason of insanity."

The legal history of the criminal insanity plea is a controversial one. It illustrates particularly well the increasingly influential role of the attorney who as defense counsel has had to decide whether and how to raise the insanity plea when representing mentally unstable or deranged clients. It also offers illuminating examples of the growing authority of the technical expert—the asylum keeper, the medical doctor, the psychiatrist—on case outcomes. Since 1800, defense attorneys and technical experts have managed to add their voices to those of judges, juries, legislators, and the ancient legal authorities in the formulation of standards and tests to determine legal insanity. These tests have gradually evolved and gained acceptance in England and the United States in the midst of continuing controversy. The twists and turns in this process illustrate the American dependence on the English common law tradition.

Although many cases, some spectacular and bizarre, comprise the elements in this process, two especially stand out: England's *McNaughton* case in 1843 and America's *Hinckley* case in 1982. The *McNaughton* case climaxed centuries of accumulating case precedents and established rules quickly adopted in America. McNaughton's defense attorney, using expert witnesses, succeeded in a novel defense that produced an acquittal and resulted in a lasting reformulation of the English standard, the McNaughton Rules.[1] In America, Hinckley's attorneys and their experts also won, and that case victory fanned old flames of controversy, forcing yet another reexamination of existing tests.[2] Neither of these two cases or any other has produced a consensus on the difficult questions involved, nor is it likely any will, as long as attorneys are free to challenge existing standards and experts can be marshalled for both prosecution and defense. The only statement on which most could agree might be the statement of the American Psychiatric Association that "the line between an [insane] irresistible impulse and a [sane] impulse not resisted is probably no sharper than between twilight and dusk."[3]

INSANITY AND THE EARLY COMMON LAW

What constitutes insanity? From ancient times to the present, theologians, doctors, and lawyers have struggled to settle on a satisfactory definition. A practical rule used in medieval England for civil purposes considered a person insane "who cannot account or number twenty pence, nor can tell who was his father or mother or how old he is."[4] Sometimes the insane were compared to children under the age of accountability, which varied from nine to fourteen. The matter became even more difficult when related to crime and more complex with the development of modern medicine, especially psychiatry and psychology in the nineteenth and twentieth centuries. All could agree that some persons were born mentally deficient, some became permanently mentally disordered, and some suffered fits of intermittent madness; all could agree that on occasions, actually very rare, such persons might commit or attempt to commit crimes. But beyond that, centuries of theological, medical, and legal thought have produced little agreement.

The Angles and Saxons who settled in England very early adopted the legal principle that *two* elements were necessary for a major crime or felony: the act itself and intent maliciously to do it. They allowed lesser penalties for acts committed by a person who might "fall out of his senses or wits."[5] When Christianity and its canon law came to England in the sixth century, it taught that people possess the freedom to choose good or evil and the ability to recognize the difference: it emphasized the importance of a person's intent. The church also taught that while some surrendered their free will to become demon-possessed, witches, warlocks, heretics or traitors, others for reasons known only to God were born or fell into madness which was itself judgment enough on them. The tradition gradually developed in which insane persons were convicted for their crimes like anyone else, but frequently, even routinely, granted royal pardons. Since they lacked sound reason (*non compos mentis*), they could not harbor malicious intent (*mens rea*).[6]

Cases involving insanity were rare and case precedent, establishing a common law tradition, accumulated very slowly. In 1212 a court decided that "the King is to be consulted about an insane man who is in prison because in his madness he confesses himself a thief while really he is not guilty." The phrase about consulting the king was apparently a legal term for the procedure allowing indefinite detention of an insane person without trial.[7] Bracton, the influential thirteenth-century judge and legal authority, listed in one of his famous notebooks a case concerning a certain Ralph, who had committed murder while "out of his wits and senses." After confessing to his deed, he was sentenced to life imprisonment instead of execution. Bracton, using the precedents known to him through reading and judicial circuit riding, wrote a section on criminal insanity in his treatise on the common law. He declared that "a crime is not committed unless the will to harm be present" and that children, animals, and madmen are incapable of having that will.[8]

Bracton's rather sophisticated analogy of insane persons to children or animals dominated English legal thought for over 400 years. Later judges, however, narrowed it to a simple, almost crude "wild beast" test that allowed acquittal for insanity only if a person were a "raving maniac" or a totally withdrawn melancholic.[9] This test made no allowance for those sometimes described as partially or temporarily insane. In Bracton's time it was not yet the practice of the courts to allow a "not guilty by reason of insanity" verdict.[10] Later authorities echoed Bracton's test when they mentioned the subject. Sir Edward Coke discussed civil proceedings relating to insanity, but scarcely touched on the criminal side. He thought that in criminal cases a madman should be treated as a child under fourteen.[11]

Sir Matthew Hale was the first English chief justice to take a serious interest in psychological theories and to try to apply them to criminal law. He distinguished natural "ideocy" or severely abnormal low intelligence from mental illness. This had two forms: permanent madness and lunacy, a type of the same with lucid intervals (caused, as many still assumed, by lunar phases). Hale thought lunacy a legitimate defense, but insisted a heavy burden of proof lay on the defendant to prove his madness at the moment of the crime. He also recognized partial insanity but was skeptical of it as a defense unless the defendant could clearly be shown to possess less understanding than a child of fourteen. No clear partial insanity defense is known to have succeeded before 1800. Hale's book, published in 1736, had more influence on judges of the eighteenth and early nineteenth centuries than any other book on the subject of insanity.[12] Since English practice before 1800 allowed no at-

torney to speak in court for a defendant, accused persons had to depend
on judges like Hale to look after their interests.

THE INSANITY DEFENSE IN EIGHTEENTH-CENTURY
ENGLAND

As late as the eighteenth century judges rarely dealt with criminal
insanity cases, hearing only one or two during their entire tenure on the
bench. There were a few cases in England which did attract widespread
attention because of the status of either the defendants or the intended
victims. These cases, therefore, were well reported and became significant precedents for the evolving criminal insanity defense.

The first fully reported case occurred in 1723 when "mad Ned" Arnold
shot, but failed to kill, Lord Onslow who he imagined was persecuting
him.[13] There was suspicion the shooting might be part of a conspiracy
to kill other public officials including King George I, so the trial was
carefully reported and widely discussed. The prosecutors emphasized
Arnold's preparations for the crime and dismissed testimony about his
erratic behavior at other times as irrelevant. No defense counsel was
allowed to speak. The judge, in his charge to the jury, imposed the
following two-part test: First, was the defendant "totally deprived of
understanding and memory, not knowing what he was doing, no more
than an infant, a brute or a wild beast," and second, was he "able to
distinguish whether he was doing good or evil... at this day when he
committed this fact." The judge warned the jurors solemnly that the
madness must be "plain and clear," because "it is not every kind of frantic
humour, or something unaccountable in a man's actions, that points him
out to be such a madman as is to be exempted from punishment." After
such a strict charge it was not surprising that the jury did not take long
to find Arnold guilty. Lord Onslow, however, obtained a royal pardon
for him. The verdict in the *Arnold* case, based on the "wild beast" test,
but mitigated by a royal pardon, was typical for that period. However,
judges soon began to regard the "right-wrong" test from *Arnold* as a
separate and unique test.

The most famous insanity defense of the eighteenth century involved
both tests. In 1760 an aristocrat, Earl Ferrers, stood trial for his life for
murdering a former employee.[14] Denied counsel, Ferrers complained
vigorously but unsuccessfully of the injustice of requiring a lunatic to
prove himself insane without assistance of counsel. At the trial the prosecution focused on Ferrers's apparent premeditation of the crime. They
quoted Hale and relied both on the wild beast test and the right-wrong
test. The prosecution claimed that Ferrers knew what he was doing as
shown by his plans, and that he knew his action was wrong as shown by
his fits of remorse immediately thereafter. They conceded that Ferrers

might be a "lunatic," but argued he was sane enough to be responsible on the day of the shooting. Ferrers pleaded "occasional Insanity of Mind" and claimed not to remember shooting anyone. As he struggled to be his own defense counsel Ferrers damaged his case by conceding that the witnesses had not proved him "so insane as not to know the Difference between a moral and an immoral Action." He insisted however that the evidence had shown him "liable to be driven and harried into that unhappy Condition upon very slight Occasions."[15] This line of defense foreshadowed the "irresistible impulse" test which would be introduced in the next century.

Ferrers also was allowed to introduce expert medical testimony, a very important new precedent. Dr. John Monro, superintendent of Bethelem Hospital for the insane in London, took the stand to define lunacy. As the usual symptoms of lunacy he offered three: "Uncommon Fury" not caused by liquor but raised by it; violence against others or self; and, above all, jealousy or suspicion without reasonable cause. He agreed that Ferrers's behavior displayed all of these symptoms but hedged when asked if lunatics when angered would still know what they were doing.[16] As a result, the long three-day trial ended with all 117 peers present voting for Ferrers's conviction. His hanging was witnessed by an enormous crowd which seemed to regard the execution of a lord for the murder of a commoner as a noteworthy triumph of English justice.

EVOLVING STANDARDS: TWO CASE PRECEDENTS

The *Arnold* and *Ferrers* cases remained the landmark cases both for England and colonial America throughout the remainder of the eighteenth and well into the nineteenth century. However, there were two significant exceptions to these precedents.[17]

The *Hadfield* case in 1800 ended in the acquittal of a person who had obviously planned the act.[18] Since Hadfield's target was King George III, whom he shot at and narrowly missed, the case attracted much attention and inspired Parliament to enact the first piece of legislation on the subject of criminal insanity. In addition, this case is the first to illustrate the potent impact of an able defense counsel on the outcome.

James Hadfield, an ex-soldier, had suffered serious head wounds in the Napoleonic Wars. He eventually returned to civilian life, married and fathered a child, but behaved irrationally on many occasions. At length his tormented mind concluded that he must end his existence and find salvation by killing the king and being executed for high treason. He obtained a pistol and shot, and lay in wait for the king at Drury Lane Theatre. When George III entered the Royal Box, Hadfield fired at him and the ball passed just a foot over the king's head. Captured by the audience, he was brought before the Duke of York, who was also present.

Hadfield calmly responded to questions and reminded the duke of his service as orderly to him during the recent war.

Six weeks later Hadfield was put on trial for treason, since an attack on the king was legally quite different from ordinary felony. The law provided more privileges to defendants in treason cases than in felonies: counsel could represent him, call and examine witnesses, and address the court. Thomas Erskine agreed to serve as Hadfield's defense counsel. Erskine, the youngest son of a Scottish lord and member of Parliament, stood at the peak of a brilliantly successful career and was reputed the highest paid and most sought after defense lawyer in England.[19] He specialized in defending political reformers and critics of high officials against charges of seditious libel and treason thrown up to silence them. He had brilliantly, if unsuccessfully, defended Tom Paine in 1792. However, in another case his logic and eloquence were so persuasive the jury acquitted the defendant without bothering to leave the jury box.

Erskine threw himself into the Hadfield defense with his usual zeal and thoroughness. He conceded that Hadfield had planned his deed, and had in some sense recognized it was wrong, since he expected to be executed for it. Although Hadfield clearly failed to meet either the wild beast or the right-wrong test, Erskine eloquently argued that those tests, if strictly applied, would in fact exclude almost anyone. The real problem for the law was temporary insanity where, as Erskine argued, "reason is not driven from her seat, but distraction sits down upon it along with her and frightens her into insane delusions." He expanded the practice of using medical experts and produced several who had examined Hadfield after the shooting. They unanimously declared his behavior was clearly due to his brain injury. One doctor had found Hadfield could answer correctly questions on a "common matter" but when any question was put to him about his delusions he answered "irrationally." Erskine skillfully distinguished his client's case from Arnold's, and Ferrers's. Arnold and Ferrers attacked men whom they knew, who were involved in real or potentially real conflict with them. Hadfield, although appearing calm the evening of the shooting, was acting under a mad delusion totally divorced from reality. Erskine still had twenty witnesses on his long list when the judges became so convinced they stopped the trial and invited the jurors to consider a special verdict of not guilty "being under the influence of insanity at the time." The judges believed the special acquittal would allow them to detain Hadfield whereas a regular "not guilty" verdict might require his release. In order to close up this legal gap Parliament hastily passed a statute recognizing such a special acquittal and providing "for the safe custody of insane persons charged with offenses."[20] The new law completely avoided the difficult task of defining insanity or the insanity defense and only provided that in such cases the judges could remand the person to indefinite detention at the king's pleasure. Hadfield remained institutionalized the rest of his life, killing a man in the hospital.[21] Erskine went on to become lord chancellor of England.

The *Hadfield* case illustrated the many variables that can affect an outcome: a wounded soldier tried in wartime, lack of any actual injury to the intended victim, attitudes of judges and jurors, perhaps even the undoubted unpopularity of King George. Above all it showed how a persuasive defense attorney, utilizing expert witnesses, could sway judges and jury to accept a new test, in this case the "delusion" test, for criminal insanity. At the time, however, the case was thought too exceptional to provide good precedent and had little immediate influence. Indeed it carried more authority in the newly independent United States of America than in England.[22]

A successful assassination only a few years after *Hadfield* again forced the English courts to consider an insanity defense. John Bellingham shot and killed the prime minister, Spencer Percival, in the lobby of the House of Commons on May 11, 1812. Bellingham, whose father had died insane, was a none-too-successful businessman. After failure of a business venture in Russia he became obsessed with a fixed notion that the British government owed him compensation for his fiasco. After months of haunting various government offices, he appealed to Percival who turned him down. Bellingham obtained pistols, waited in the place where Percival regularly passed in the Commons Lobby and shot him dead at point-blank range. He was rushed to trial only four days later before Lord Chief Justice Mansfield and two other high-ranking justices with the attorney general himself and a battery of government lawyers as prosecutors. The court appointed defense counsel one day before the trial and refused him time to seek experts or otherwise prepare the case. During the trial the prosecution used the *Arnold* and *Ferrers* cases, suggesting that although both had behaved at times insanely, they were found sane enough at the time of their crimes to be convicted. The defense tried to show that Bellingham had behaved erratically ever since returning from Russia and had a mad delusion about the obligation of the government to reimburse him. Lord Mansfield, in his charge to the jury, brushed off the defendant's general state of mind as "perfectly immaterial." Not troubling to suppress his personal sense of loss of the "amiable" Percival, he offered the jury only the wild beast and right-wrong tests in strictest form. Small wonder that following such a charge the jury decided on a guilty verdict. Only eight days elapsed from the crime to a hasty execution![23]

THE INSANITY DEFENSE IN COLONIAL AMERICA AND THE EARLY REPUBLIC

Englishmen carried with them their common law precedents on insanity when they colonized North America. It appears that insane persons were usually dealt with extra-legally in the colonial period.[24] Only a few American doctors, like Dr. Benjamin Rush, took an interest in care and treatment of the insane. Dr. Rush, the famous Philadelphia physician and signer of the Declaration of Independence, pioneered in more humane treatment of the insane and more careful study of the many types of insanity. In 1812 he wrote a very influential book on the subject summarizing his views near the end of his long career in England and America. In this book he argued that the insane be treated gently, not be put on public display and never be whipped.[25] He did not discuss the insanity defense in criminal cases, however.

In the early decades of the Republic insanity pleas were rare. When they occurred, the courts closely followed English precedents even though doctors were beginning to question them. Dr. Isaac Ray (1807–1881) lamented in his 1838 book that:

Criminal trials in which insanity is pleaded in defense are generally so little known beyond the place of their occurrence, that it is difficult to ascertain on what particular principles of the common law the decisions of the courts have been founded, though from all that can be gathered, their practice, like that of the British, has been diverse and fluctuating.[26]

Ray further complained that instead of utilizing new medical knowledge American courts slavishly followed the "loose and vacillating" practice of English courts and their "old maxims." He considered it unfortunate that the unique precedent of the *Hadfield* case was little followed.

Dr. Ray's contribution, however, was not so much his critique of contemporary legal practice, as his carefully reasoned appeal, based on his medical expertise, for a broader legal interpretation of insanity in criminal cases. He insisted that criminal responsibility be decided on the question: Was the act a product of mental disorder or defect? His book prospered through five editions in the United States and one in England during his lifetime and he lived to commend New Hampshire for adopting his "product rule" in 1869.[27] Ray thought that the "wild beast" and the "knowledge of right and wrong" tests were antiquated and overly narrow, but they continued to be the main standards in American courts.

A study of twelve criminal cases with insanity defense between 1816 and 1841 has demonstrated that the "right and wrong" test remained the main test used, with the temporary insanity plea gaining some acceptance.[28] Three of these twelve cases ended in acquittals. In nine cases the defendants were found guilty with three of these being executed. Of the last six cases, the temporary insanity defense worked to mitigate some of the sentences imposed. Such was the case of the Italian immigrant indicted in New York City for assault and battery: he bit and tore off the tip of his wife's nose. Defense counsel in the case argued that his client had become so deranged at the time that he "had not a mind capacitated for distinguishing good and evil." The jury finding him guilty, nevertheless recommended mercy. The judge, however, did sentence him to two years in prison.[29] The temporary insanity plea had partially succeeded. Its first major acceptance, however, came in the *Lawrence* case.

In 1835 a certain Richard Lawrence accosted President Andrew Jackson in the rotunda of the U.S. Capitol and attempted to fire two pistols at him at close range. Fortunately for Jackson the caps of both pistols failed to ignite the powder and they misfired. Lawrence was tried, the prosecutor being Francis Scott Key of poetic fame. The defense counsel here successfully raised the insanity defense with the judge reminding the jury of the *Hadfield* verdict. It only took the jury five minutes to find the deluded Lawrence "not guilty, he having been under the influence of insanity at the time he committed the act."[30] These case examples illustrate that behavior suggesting temporary insanity on the part of the accused occasionally could win a verdict of acquittal or at least mitigation of the sentence.

ENGLAND'S LANDMARK CASE: *McNAUGHTON*

Meanwhile in England the convictions of Bellingham and others had shown that Hadfield's acquittal had not produced much effect. Important changes were, however, occurring in both the legal and medical climate. Prison doctors were being appointed and their opinions on insanity sought and respected. The number of capital offenses was greatly reduced and the courts allowed defendants in all felony and even misdemeanor cases to be represented by counsel. The insanity plea was still rare, but its success rate was slowly increasing as both doctors and lawyers questioned the old precedents about insanity.[31]

One notable example occurred in 1840, after Edward Oxford fired two pistols at Queen Victoria.[32] At the trial his defense counsel skillfully pointed out that madness ran in Oxford's family and called five medical experts who "all gave it as their decided opinion that he was of unsound mind." The jury found him, "not guilty, he being insane at the time."

The most sensational and significant criminal insanity trial to occur in nineteenth-century England was that of Daniel McNaughton. The definitions of legal insanity it occasioned, the so-called McNaughton Rules, were quickly adopted in England and America and remain to this very day the standard test for insanity in about half of the American states and a major portion of tests in nearly all others.[33] On January 20, 1843, McNaughton fired a pistol at Edward Drummond, private secretary to the prime minister, Sir Robert Peel, mortally wounding him. Obsessed and tortured with delusions of persecution, McNaughton apparently sought to escape or end them by killing the prime minister, but shot his secretary by mistake.

McNaughton had suffered obvious mental problems for at least five years. He complained to acquaintances of pains in his head and of people spying on him day and night. Later he spoke of a "parcel of devils" following him and purchased pistols. At times he seemed normal, but his appearance and behavior became progressively more eccentric until friends advised his father to put him "under restraint." He repeatedly visited law enforcement officials, making rambling, almost unintelligible complaints and asking for help. At length he focused on the Tory political party and their leader, Sir Robert Peel, as the chief enemy. McNaughton came up behind Peel's secretary in broad daylight on a busy street and fired a pistol shot into him at close range. He pulled out a second pistol and was barely prevented from shooting him again by a policeman who ran across the street and grabbed him. The man died five days later. A psychiatrist today would likely diagnose McNaughton as suffering from paranoid schizophrenia with a psychosis characterized by a host of paranoid delusions.[34] Doctors of his day diagnosed his case as "monomania," a form characterized by insane delusions or behavior relating to one subject, but apparent sanity on others.

McNaughton, like Hadfield, benefitted from the service of one of the most brilliant and successful lawyers of the day. This was Alexander Cockburn, who came from a well-connected Scottish aristocratic family. Although only forty-one, Cockburn was already a queen's counsel and had earned many academic and legal honors. He was known as a clever, successful, defense attorney who enjoyed unusual cases which presented opportunities to make new law. Parties in his cases during a long and distinguished career would range from archbishops to racehorses. Cockburn seemed determined from the outset to use McNaughton's case to set a new precedent to extend the limits of the insanity defense. *Hadfield* established a precedent for a successful insanity defense even when the defendant, knowing right from wrong, nevertheless committed the crime. Cockburn built on this and argued that a person appearing otherwise sane might be possessed by such an "uncontrollable delusion" that he would believe himself justified in doing what he knew would otherwise be wrong. A person so deluded deserved acquittal by reason of insanity if he committed a crime as a direct offspring of that delusion. Cockburn held up Isaac Ray's book in court and pronounced it "perhaps the most scientific treatise" of the age on insanity and used it to refute the old reservations of Hale and others about "partial insanity." He then produced medical experts, including Dr. Munro from Bethleham Hospital and the influential Dr. Forbes Winslow, a well-known author of a book on criminal insanity. Dr. Munro made a significant impression when he pronounced McNaughton insane after examining him, but Dr. Winslow created a sensation when Cockburn led him to declare emphatically that the defendant was insane although Winslow had only observed him in the courtroom and had never once even spoken to him. The judges were so impressed they stopped the case. Chief Justice Tindall intimated to prosecution and jury that "the whole of the medical evidence is on one side." The jurors quickly agreed and found McNaughton "not guilty on the ground of insanity." He was institutionalized until his death in 1865.[35]

The acquittal stirred a storm of indignation throughout England including Queen Victoria herself. If one would-be assassin of the queen (Oxford) and another would-be assassin of her chief minister were allowed to escape the gallows so easily, would this not encourage more attempts? Were not all criminals partially insane in some sense? *The Times*, the leading London newspaper, demanded to know "where sanity ends and madness begins."[36] The uproar reverberated to the House of Lords, England's highest judicial body. The lords called before them all the judges of the high courts and asked them to respond collectively to questions about the state of the law on insanity. The questions and the judges' replies (here abbreviated) deserve careful attention:

Question 1: "What is the law respecting alleged crimes committed by persons afflicted with insane delusion?"

Answer: "A person under the influence of an insane delusion . . . is nevertheless punishable . . . if he knew at the time of committing the crime he was acting contrary to law, i.e., the law of the land."

Question 2: "What are the proper questions to be submitted to the jury when a person alleged to be afflicted with insane delusion is charged . . . and insanity is set up as a defense?"

Question 3: "In what terms ought the question to be left to the jury as to the prisoner's state of mind at the time when the act was committed?"

Answers for both questions 2 and 3: "The jurors ought to be told . . . that every man is presumed to be sane, . . . until the contrary be proved . . . and that to establish a defense of insanity, it must be clearly proved that at the time . . . the party accused was laboring under such a defect of reason, from disease of the mind, as not to know the nature and quality of the act he was doing; or if he did know it, that he did not know he was doing what was wrong."

Question 4: "If a person under an insane delusion as to existing fact commits an offense in consequence thereof, is he thereby excused?"

Answer: "He must be considered in the same situation as to responsibility as if the facts with respect to which the delusion exists were real." The example given was a man killing another under the delusion his own life was directly threatened.

Question 5: "Can a medical man . . . who never saw the prisoner previously to the trial, but who was present during the whole trial . . . be asked his opinion as to the state of the prisoner's mind at the time of the crime?"

Answer: "We think the medical man . . . cannot in strictness be asked his opinion
in the terms above stated. But where the facts are undisputed, and the
question becomes one of science only, it may be convenient to allow the
question to be put in that general form."[37]

Chief Justice Tindall, who had presided at the McNaughton trial,
presented these answers as the view of all but one of the high court
judges. Their lordships found the answers quite satisfactory and no one
was so impolite as to ask Tindall how McNaughton himself could have
been acquitted under such an interpretation. His delusion concerned
harassment or persecution, but not such an immediate threat to life as
to require shooting to kill.

The McNaughton Rules satisfied the English because they did not
depart from settled law. They combined the two standard tests, and
recognized, though with strict limits, the existence of insane delusions.
They also gave clear guidance about how to charge a jury. The case itself
offers another clear example of the decisive role an able defense lawyer
can play, especially when he can expertly marshall technical experts to
his cause. McNaughton's lawyer, Cockburn, rose to knighthood, Parliament, attorney general, and finally became the Lord Chief Justice of
England.

THE McNAUGHTON RULES IN AMERICA

The McNaughton Rules appealed to U.S. courts also. They did not
represent some major departure, and they offered a more precise restatement of standard practice. In the absence of statutes on the subject
they provided valuable legitimation.[38] Massachusetts, which seemed to
have more than its share of criminal insanity cases, was first to adopt
the Rules. Within a year the Massachusetts supreme court was citing
McNaughton as authority for applying the right-wrong test in *Commonwealth v. Rogers*.[39] Nearly all states soon followed and by 1864 the Rules
had crossed the Mississippi, traversed the Great Plains, scaled the Rock-
ies, and were being cited all the way to California.[40] Only New Hampshire
rejected all explicit tests except the "product rule," insisting in an 1871
case that "the only question to be determined was whether the criminal
act was a product of mental disorder or defect."[41]

No other state followed New Hampshire; moreover, even those courts
that criticized the McNaughton Rules tended to apply narrowing or
broadening interpretations of them. Some carefully narrowed the Rules
to the issue of a knowledge of the legality of the specific act, rather than
of a moral right or wrong. Bound by such a narrow view, not even the
best defense lawyer could successfully defend a man like Albert Fish
who tortured, murdered, and actually ate children. Fish apparently knew

murder was illegal but believed he had some overriding command from God; he was judged sane enough to be convicted.[42] Many defense lawyers argued, however, that courts should consider the extent a person might lose control of the will, as well as be knowledgable of right and wrong. After all, English attorneys had won the acquittal of Hadfield and McNaughton. Some U.S. courts began to broaden the Rules to allow the so-called "irresistible impulse" test and by the 1880s it was well established in several states with considerable support from medical opinion.[43]

Those who liked the irresistible impulse test remained in the minority, however, in both England and America. Opponents of this test argued that there was probably no such separate mental illness as a disordered will or if such existed it was impossible to prove in court. Society could not allow it because any criminal might claim it. Finally, there was no common law precedent or statutory authority for such a test. Nevertheless, by the mid-twentieth century fourteen states included irresistible impulse with the other accepted tests.

A successful presidential assassination in 1881 demonstrated the uncertainty of any defense based on an insanity plea. Charles Guiteau shot and mortally wounded President Garfield, believing the act a "sad necessity," that would "unite the Republican Party and save the Republic."[44] Guiteau's family tree abounded with cousins, aunts, and uncles who were deranged, as was a sister. A political pamphleteer, Guiteau was convinced that his services were so valuable to the Republican Party that they would reward him with a diplomatic appointment. Frustrated when this was not forthcoming, he concluded Garfield was the obstacle to his destiny and laid careful plans to "remove" him. Guiteau's preparations included revision of his book for the sales he anticipated after the shooting, inspection of the jail to which he expected to go, and purchase of an ivory-handled pistol he thought suitable for museum display. After shadowing the president for weeks and postponing the act once because Mrs. Garfield was present, and again because it was too hot, Guiteau finally found both nerve and opportunity. He successfully fired two bullets into the president at point-blank range. Although he failed to get to the cab he had waiting to take him to jail, he did escape the lynching he feared and was tried for his deed.

The trial of Guiteau lasted from November 1881 to January 1882 and assumed almost a circus atmosphere. There was no stellar defense attorney willing to defend the unpopular Guiteau. This task fell to his brother-in-law, Scoville, a real estate lawyer quite inexperienced in criminal law. The judge gave the widest latitude, especially to the prosecution. Guiteau, for his part, interjected irrelevant and bizarre comments. Both sides called numerous medical experts with the prosecution's experts defending a narrow interpretation of the McNaughton Rules, while the defense experts advocated a broader interpretation. Although several doctors who had known Guiteau for years declared him insane, the jury agreed with the prosecution's experts—and with the irate general public—that there was "too much method in his madness" and found him guilty. He was hanged.[45] The *Guiteau* case illustrated the limits of defense counsel's powers of persuasion and of expert opinion. In cases where the victim was popular and public opinion aroused, the insanity defense would likely fail.

The U.S. Congress and Supreme Court were not eager to attempt definitions of the scope and limit of the insanity plea. The Court did accept the McNaughton Rules when, in *Davis v. U.S.*, (1895)[46] it dealt with the burden of proof question. The Court here held that "in a prosecution for murder, the defense being insanity . . . [a defendant] is entitled to an acquittal of the specific crime charged if, upon all the evidence there is reasonable doubt whether he was capable *in law* of committing the crime." The Court then explained the test being used. The defendant's lawyer need not prove his client's insanity—and thus his legal innocence—beyond a reasonable doubt. The defense, moreover, need not offer a preponderance of proof, or even equal evidence to balance against the prosecution's proofs. A reasonable doubt in the jury's mind was sufficient to defeat the prosecution which, for its part, must prove sanity and guilt *beyond a reasonable doubt* on *all points* in the case. Mr. Justice Harlan, writing for the Court, reviewed the history of the criminal insanity defense and cited English precedents and authorities. Harlan affirmed the McNaughton Rules and the right-wrong test. Evaluating the burden of proof question—who had to prove sanity/insanity— Harlan conceded that the "accused is bound to produce some evidence that will impair or weaken" the presumption of sanity. However, he insisted that in a murder case no one would wish "to disregard the humane principle existing at common law" that to make a crime "cognisable by human laws there must be both a will and an act." Reversing the conviction in *Davis* on the burden of proof question, the U.S. Supreme Court at the same time affirmed the McNaughton Rules and firmly incorporated them into American law. The state courts were already using the McNaughton Rules, but only about half followed the Supreme Court on the burden of proof ruling. Judges in all the other states continued to adhere to the older English precedents which required a "preponderance of evidence" to prove insanity.

TWENTIETH-CENTURY CHALLENGES TO McNAUGHTON

Challenges to the McNaughton Rules and experiments in revising them continued sporadically in the twentieth century, but change in legal definitions came slowly if at all. The medical community, particularly psychiatrists could reach no consensus, but did indeed change their views. They deleted the word "insanity" from the medical vocabulary and substituted a myriad of new terms they considered more precise and more useful. Some courts responded to changing medical opinion by devising two new tests intended to allow fuller use of medical expertise. These challenges to the older tests soon encountered difficulties as other courts continued to uphold some version of the McNaughton Rules. The District of Columbia Court of Appeals tried to devise a new test in the 1954 *Durham* case.[47] Dissatisfied with the failure of the insanity defense, the court reversed the conviction of petty thief, Monty Durham, not once but twice until his third trial ended in acquittal by reason of insanity. Appellate Judge David Bazelon wrote the court's opinion stating that the only criminal insanity test should be whether the alleged crime was the product of mental disease or defect.

Advocates of the "Durham Rule" or "Product Rule," as it was called, believed that abandoning the McNaughton Rules for a simpler test would allow greater flexibility and more attention to medical expertise, and thus ensure fairness. They noted it was essentially the same as the New Hampshire test, in use since 1870. What seemed admirable simplicity to some was too vague or too generous to others. Thus most judges continued to prefer McNaughton and ultimately the *Durham* experiment was abandoned entirely in the 1972 *Brawner* case.[48]

Meanwhile the California Supreme Court experimented on another modification of the McNaughton Rules: the legal conception of diminished responsibility. This allowed consideration for any sort of mental disability relevant to the crime for the purpose of reducing the gravity of the crime. Thus a person whose mind could be proven to be "partially disabled," who killed a person, might be found guilty of manslaughter instead of murder. However, by 1979 only fifteen other states had adopted some version of the diminished capacity approach.[49] Judges in most states and the District of Columbia rejected it as an area needing legislative clarification. The British Parliament showed more interest in taking action than American legislators and incorporated a form of "diminished responsibility" into the Homicide Act of 1957 in Britain.

The Missouri State Supreme Court resisted another challenge to *McNaughton* in *State v. McGee* (1950).[50] McGee was convicted of first degree murder under the McNaughton Rules. His defense attorney, appealing the verdict, challenged the right-wrong test as unconstitutional because it denied due process, equal protection, and allowed cruel and unusual punishment of a person who by other standards would be acquitted by reason of insanity. The state supreme court dismissed this challenge to the constitutionality of *McNaughton*. Noting that the test was "of judicial origin arising out of the common law," the state court upheld it because it had been consistently followed in the state since

1855. Such long usage, without challenge, reinforced a strong presumption of constitutionality.

Thus the two major American efforts to modify the English precedents, the Durham test and the doctrine of diminished capacity, made little impact. Resistance remained strong. By the 1970s judges in two-thirds of the states continued to formulate their instructions to the juries in terms of the McNaughton Rules, while judges in the other third used the Rules plus some version of "irresistible impulse" until two sensational cases, the Dan White case in San Francisco in 1978 and the John Hinckley case in Washington, D.C. in 1982 attracted national attention and again provoked debate on the criminal insanity defense.

PRELUDE TO HINCKLEY: THE DAN WHITE CASE

Dan White, the San Francisco city supervisor who shot and killed Mayor George Moscone and fellow supervisor Harvey Milk, certainly appeared to be no madman or deluded misfit. He served successfully as a soldier, policeman, and fireman for many years before being elected to the Board of Supervisors in 1977. White quickly found his idealism challenged in the real world of everyday big-city politics. He offered the mayor his resignation as supervisor, but ten days later changed his mind and attempted to withdraw his resignation. The mayor seemed agreeable but in the days that followed a legal and political dispute developed over whether the resignation could be withdrawn or White somehow reappointed. Harvey Milk, a political opponent and leader of the gay community, especially shocked White by urging the city attorney to rule it legally impossible for White to withdraw his resignation or be reappointed. White became convinced both Moscone and Milk had betrayed and deceived him. He armed himself and went to city hall, avoiding the front door where a metal detector would have revealed his gun. After a short conversation White fired four bullets into the mayor, killing him instantly. He then reloaded the revolver and repeated his performance in Milk's office. White's attorney produced four psychiatrists who had interviewed White and concluded that he was mentally ill and not responsible for his actions. They testified he was not capable of harboring malice and premeditating murder because of severe depression. Defense counsel's dramatic emphasis on White's sudden affection for large quantities of junk food inspired newspapers to call it the "Twinkie" defense. White had not behaved as a wild beast, he was under no insane delusion, and in some sense he knew he was doing wrong, as evidenced by his quick surrender and confession afterwards. Perhaps an irresistible impulse overpowered him? In any case the jury viewed him very sympathetically and accepted the diminished capacity defense. White was found guilty of voluntary manslaughter, not murder, and sentenced to seven years and eight months in prison. The mild sentence produced riotous street scenes in San Francisco and the California legislature passed a bill intended to abolish diminished responsibility as a defense. Again, the whole complicated question of criminal insanity had become a subject of intense public debate and again an able defense counsel and medical experts had convinced a jury. White was paroled in 1984 after serving five years. He never resumed a normal life, committing suicide in October 1985.[51]

McNAUGHTON AND HINCKLEY

The controversy over the Dan White case had scarcely died away before the whole nation was shocked by a presidential assassination attempt and another sensational trial featuring an insanity defense. On March 30, 1981, John W. Hinckley, Jr., shot and nearly killed President Ronald Reagan.

John Hinckley, Jr.'s background contained elements that would later be significant for his insanity defense.[52] He developed a withdrawn personality during his high school and college years. He spent more and more time alone, fantasizing about great successes in music, in politics, or some undetermined field. In the spring of 1976 he dropped out of college and moved to Hollywood, California, hoping to sell songs he was writing. Rejected and disappointed, he began reading anti-Semitic and racist literature. Continually begging for money, he wrote his parents about nonexistent successes and a nonexistent girlfriend. In the late 1970s and early 1980s Hinckley's life took on an increasingly frenetic pace as he moved and traveled almost constantly. He bought guns, practiced shooting, and wrote poems, A psychologist who happened to meet him thought the twenty-five-year old acted more like fourteen: He was taking antidepressants to combat suicidal tendencies. After repeated viewings of the movie *Taxi Driver* he came to identify with the "hero," a friendless, lonely man, who while plotting to kill a presidential candidate, meets and rescues a child prostitute, played by Jodie Foster. The frustrated, embittered, and perhaps mentally ailing Hinckley began to act out the movie script in his own way. Finding Ms. Foster, Hinckley followed her to Yale, vainly besieging her with calls and letters. He finally resolved to do an "historical deed, to gain your respect and love," as he wrote her, just before leaving his hotel room to shoot the president.[53]

Hinckley waited for the president outside the Washington Hilton and as soon as Reagan appeared fired the six "Devastator" bullets in his pistol very rapidly. One bullet hit Press Secretary Brady, another a policeman, another a Secret Service agent, and another ricocheted off the car and hit the president in the chest, lodging just inches from his heart. The agent who first reached Hinckley recalled that he was still clicking the weapon as he was knocked to the ground.

Hinckley's wealthy parents quickly rallied to his aid and employed a first-rate Washington law firm, Williams and Connolly, to defend him. This firm, noted for success in criminal cases involving white-collar defendants, deployed a senior partner, Vincent J. Fuller, a junior partner, Lon Babby, and two associates to handle the case. Fuller, fifty-one years old, had earned his law degree from Georgetown University and had twenty-five years of experience as an expert trial lawyer. Babby, thirty-one years old, was a 1976 Yale Law School graduate. Conservative estimates of the costs for attorney fees and the battery of experts for the defense ran from half a million to a million dollars.[54]

Hinckley's trial was scheduled in a District of Columbia court.[55] Although under direct federal control with presidentially appointed judges, the District has its own special laws and own case law. In 1970 Congress had passed a special act for the District only, using the definition of the American Law Institute's Model Penal Code for criminal insanity. This was a slightly revised version of the McNaughton Rules.[56] In 1972 the D.C. Court of Appeals had set up the so-called Brawner Rule, which provided that a person is not responsible if, as a result of mental disease or defect, he lacks "substantial capacity to appreciate the wrongfulness of his conduct or to conform his conduct to the requirements of the law."

The replacement of "knowledge" by "appreciate" in this version of the McNaughton right-wrong test was intended to allow acquittal if the defendant knew right from wrong, but his mind was so disordered he was unable to appreciate the difference emotionally. The "conform his conduct" point expanded the notion of "irresistible impulse" to general incapacity for self-control. However, another section explicitly excluded repeated criminal acts or general antisocial behavior as evidence of insanity.

Intensive preparation and legal maneuvering preceded the Hinckley trial. Both sides recruited experts and sought pretrial rulings from Judge Barrington Parker that would benefit their case. Defense counsel proposed that "diminished responsibility" be introduced as an option, but the judge refused, citing lack of precedent, They also proposed to exclude the testimony of the government's psychiatrists on the grounds that their opinion of Hinckley's mental state on March 30, 1981 had been tainted by his post-arrest behavior and statements. The judge again refused. The defense did win a big—perhaps a decisive—victory on the burden of proof question. Some of the thirteen counts against Hinckley were federal, some local. Federal precedent since *Davis* required that once the insanity plea was raised the burden of proof was on the prosecution to prove the defendant was sane at the moment of the crime, while in the District the burden was on the defense to show that a preponderance of evidence indicated the defendant was not sane at that time. Defense counsel convinced the judge that any attempt to divide the burden of proof would be too confusing and that in a mixed case the federal standard should prevail to protect the defendant's rights. When the trial opened, then, the defense had put the prosecution into the unenviable position of having to prove beyond a reasonable doubt that Hinckley had been sane enough on the day of the shooting to be found guilty.[57]

The Hinckley trial lasted nearly seven weeks. Chief Prosecutor Roger Adelman portrayed Hinckley as a lazy, fame-seeking, manipulative, privileged loner who had calmly spent an entire year thinking about which high-publicity crime he should commit. Defense counsel, for their part, called four distinguished experts to the stand. These included Dr. William Carpenter, director of the Maryland Psychiatric Research Center; Dr. Michael Bear, assistant professor of psychiatry at Harvard Medical School, an internationally known neurologist with special interest in brain disorders and human behavior; Dr. Ernst Prelinger, a Yale psychologist; and Dr. Michael Goldman, a forensic psychiatrist. They testified that Hinckley suffered from a major depressive disorder and from process schizophrenia. This is a mental illness that begins in adolescence and progresses in severity. It includes delusions such as the belief that events—Reagan in a crowd or Foster in a movie—were happening just for the afflicted person. The government's psychiatrists offered a much less severe diagnosis: a depressive neurosis with only borderline passive-aggressive features such as secretiveness, jealousy, failure to accept social norms, and inability to sustain consistent work behavior. Dr. Sally Johnson, the court-appointed doctor who had interviewed Hinckley extensively believed his neurosis mild; he remained sane enough to be responsible for his actions.[58] However, after much dispute the defense counsel persuaded the court to admit Hinckley's CAT scan, a new medical technique never before allowed in evidence. It showed deformities of the brain which some but by no means all medical experts regarded as evidence of schizophrenia.

The testimony finally concluded and the judge charged the jury, using the Brawner Rule. The prosecution must have proved that Hinkley possessed substantial capacity to appreciate the wrongness of his conduct and knowledge to conform his conduct to the requirement of the law. In addition, he stated that the burden of proof was on the prosecution to prove beyond a reasonable doubt that on the date of the crime the defendant was *not* suffering from mental disease or defect. After three days the jury brought in a verdict of not guilty by reason of insanity on all thirteen counts.

The acquittal on all counts surprised nearly everyone, even Hinckley

himself, and provoked a storm of controversy reminiscent of the reac-
tions to the McNaughton verdict in England. Hinckley had even composed a speech to be read at his sentencing.[59] Instead he was sent to St.
Elizabeth's hospital for detention in the mental ward. Prominent newspapers printed articles asserting that the insanity defense had "gone
bonkers," and Attorney General Meese led the hue and cry to abolish
it altogether.[60] The U.S. Congress reacted swiftly to the outcry as had
the British Parliament in 1843. Congress had never in the 206 years of
the Republic legislated on the insanity defense, but now speedily opened
hearings on the subject. In the heat of the moment it seemed not to
matter that the use of the insanity defense was rare and insanity acquittals
rarer still; moreover the great bulk of cases were in state courts which
would not be affected by federal legislation.

In England the House of Lords, after a debate full of criticisms of the
McNaughton verdict, had exercised its right to summon the judges of the
high courts to answer pointed questions on the subject. Lacking this legal
authority, the U.S. senators used other powers they possessed. The Subcommittee on Criminal Law of the Senate Committee on the Judiciary
invited the Hinckley jurors to appear voluntarily to explain their actions.
Just three days after the jury's verdict this subcommittee had before it
five proposed pieces of legislation limiting the insanity defense and five
of the Hinckley jurors, including the foreman, in its presence.[61] The
senators claimed not to be questioning the verdict, but seeking help to
frame legislation on the insanity defense. Some senators had reservations
about dissecting a verdict; others indirectly pressed the jurors to support
new legislation and to admit the verdict set a precedent for a too liberal
insanity defense. Senators lectured jurors on the history of the subject,
including the McNaughton Rules which they noted were, in various
forms, the law of the land.

The jurors' responses were illuminating if not very helpful. They said
that they had listened carefully to all the psychiatrists. Just as Justice
Potter Stewart had difficulty defining pornography, but knew it when
he saw it, they had trouble defining insanity but knew it when they saw
it and had seen it clearly enough in Hinckley. The arguments of the
defense attorney and the opinions of the experts had weighed heavily
with them. "All the psychiatrists found there was a mental disorder,"
one juror had told a reporter.[62] After the testimony was all in, "we went
in and we argued," recalled one of them. "We knew that the gentleman
was guilty of his act, but we also knew there was a mental problem."
Some jurors would have preferred an option of guilty but mentally ill,
but complained "we could not do any better than we did on account of
your forms."[63]

The senators and representatives as well as many state legislators decided that future juries should have more guidance and stricter stan-

dards when they face the insanity plea. The U.S. Congress passed the Comprehensive Crime Control Act of 1984 which provided that in federal cases "the defendant has the burden of proving the defense of insanity by clear and convincing evidence."[64]

The provisions of this act were a reversion to a narrower construction of the McNaughton right-wrong test, emphasizing cognition and virtually excluding deficiencies in "will-power" or self-control. Congress rejected the *mens rea* test urged by Senator Joseph Biden of Delaware which would concede insanity only if it could be proven the accused lacked the "state of mind necessary to commit the offense charged." As Biden had explained to the Hinckley jurors, if a man choked his wife to death not realizing at all what he was doing—believing for example he was "squeezing lemons," he could qualify. But if he knew it was his wife, his hands and her neck, he was legally sane.[65] This would seem to be essentially a reversion to Bracton's medieval "wild beast" test. No laws were passed adopting Biden's test, but by 1984 eight states had legislated the option of guilty but mentally ill. This allowed a jury to bring in a guilty verdict but required prison authorities to provide the accused with psychiatric treatment. Since prison authorities were doing this anyway this change proved to be more cosmetic than significant. Among the other states about half held to the American Legal Institute Code and half to the older and usually stricter right-wrong test, sometimes with "irresistible impulse." Only two states, Idaho and Montana, allowed no insanity defense at all. The U.S. Supreme Court reinforced the trend to "tighten up" on those pleading insanity when in 1983 it ruled constitutional the detention of a person adjudged "not guilty by reason of insanity" in a mental hospital longer than the maximum prison term to which he or she would have been sentenced if found guilty.[66] This followed the tradition English practice of leaving the criminally insane to indefinite detention at the "King's pleasure."

CONCLUSIONS

Use of the insanity plea in criminal cases continues to be rare and its success rate is not high. Not more than one in four who attempt this defense are successful and only 1 to 2 percent are set free. Fewer than 4,000 persons were detained in mental hospitals in a recent year because they had been adjudged "not guilty by reason of insanity," while the total prison population was approaching half a million.[67] The debate continues and doubtless will continue between lawyers and doctors, among judges, legislators, and the public, especially when excited by actions of a Ferrers, a Hadfield, a McNaughton, a Guiteau, a Dan White, or a Hinckley. Over the centuries courts in England, then in America too, have dealt with this issue on a case-by-case basis in the common law tradition. Defense attorneys, as soon as they gained the right to represent their clients in court, exerted great influence in swaying judges and juries. Their greatest successes have come as they have mobilized technical experts. Defense counsels and their experts have repeatedly joined battle with prosecutors and their experts and have challenged the courts to reconsider and readjust legal tests and procedures. Sensational cases have aroused public opinion and pushed legislators on occasion to intervene also.

American ingenuity, both legal and medical, has produced few refinements in the traditional English common law insanity tests; radical departures have generally failed. Indeed, it is not too much to conclude that in America today in the federal and state courts criminal insanity is determined either by the English rules, slightly revised or by the English rules, slightly more revised.

NOTES

1. William Winslade and Judith Ross, *The Insanity Plea* (New York: Charles Scribern's Sons, 1983), p. 199.

2. Herbert Fingarette, *The Meaning of Criminal Insanity* (Berkeley: University of California Press, 1972), p. 12.

3. Lincoln Caplan, *The Insanity Defense and the Trial of John W. Hinckley, Jr.* (Boston: Godine, 1984), p. 120.

4. Quoted from a sixteenth-century source in Francis B. Sayre, "*Mens Rea*," 45 *Harvard Law Review* 5 (1932), pp. 1,005–6.

5. From a manuscript dated 1000 A.D. or earlier ascribed to Archbishop Egbert of York, quoted in Nigel Walker, *Crime and Insanity in England*, vol. 1, *The Historical Perspective* (Edinburgh: University Press, 1968), p. 15.

6. Sayre, "*Mens Rea*," pp. 985–86.

7. F. W. Maitland, eds. *Select Pleas of the Crown* (London: Quaritch, 1888), Case 613, pp. 66–67.

8. Henry de Bracton, *De Legibus et Consuetudinibus Angliae* (On the Laws and Customs of England) edited by George E. Woodbine, translated by Samuel E. Thorne, 4 vols. (Cambridge, MA: Belnap Press of Harvard, 1968–1977), vol. 2, p. 424.

9. Anthony M. Platt, "The Origins and Development of the 'Wild Beast' Concept of Mental Illness and Its Relation to Theories of Criminal Responsibility," *Issues in Criminology*, vol. 1, no. 1 (Fall 1965), pp. 4–5.

10. Walker, *Crime and Insanity*, pp. 26–28.

11. Edward Coke, *The Third Part of the Institutes of the Laws of England* (London: E & R Brooke, 1797), Chapter 1, note 7.

12. Matthew Hale, *History of the Pleas of the Crown* (1736), vol. 1, p. 34. Walker, *Crime and Insanity* p. 35.

13. Rex v. Arnold, T. B. Howell, ed., *State Trials*, 33 vols. (London: 1816–1828), vol. 16, 698–766.

14. Rex v. Ferrers, ibid., vol. 10, 477–516.

15. Ibid., p. 507.

16. Ibid., p. 508.

17. Another exception was the obscure case of Miss Broadric who was found not guilty by reason of insanity and institutionalized for killing her ex-lover in 1795. *The Times* (London), 18 July, 1795, p. 3. Reprinted in Walker, *Crime and Insanity*, Appendix F.

18. Rex v. Hadfield, Howell, ed. *State Trials*, vol. 27, 1,281–1,352.

19. Sir Leslie Stephen and Sir Sidney Lee, eds., *Dictionary of National Biography*, vol. 6 (London: Oxford University Press, 1921), pp. 853–61.

20. 40 George III c. 96.

21. Walker, *Crime and Insanity*, pp. 78–81.

22. See the Lawrence Case, below.

23. The Bellingham Case is published in an addendum in George D. Collinson, *A Treatise on the Law Concerning Idiots, Lunatics and Other Perons Non Compotes Mentis* (London: W. Reed, 1812), pp. 636–74.

24. Petitions by "sundry inhabitants" to the Pennsylvania Assembly for the establishment of a hospital, January 23, 1751, printed in Thomas Morton, *The History of the Pennsylvania Hospital, 1751–1895* (Philadelphia: Times Printing House, 1897), p. 8.

25. Thomas Szaz, ed., *The Age of Madness: The History of Involuntary Mental Hospitalization Presented in Selected Texts* (Garden City, NY: Doubleday, 1973), pp. 12–14.

26. Isaac Ray, *A Treatise on the Medical Jurisprudence of Insanity* (Boston: Little, Brown, 1838; Cambridge, MA: Belknap Press, 1962), p. 47.

27. Ibid., p. ix.

28. Anthony Platt and Bernard L. Diamond, "The Origins of the 'Right and Wrong' Test of Criminal Responsibility and Its Subsequent Development in the United States: An Historical Survey" in 54 *California Law Review* (1966), pp. 1,250–58.

29. Ibid., pp. 1,252–53.

30. Trial Report in *Niles Register* 48, (April 18, 1835), pp. 119–25. See also Richard C. Rohrs, "Partisan Politics and the Attempted Assassination of Andrew Jackson" in 1 *Journal of the Early Republic* (1981), pp. 149–63.

31. Donald West and Alexander Walk, eds., *Daniel McNaughton: His Trial and the Aftermath* (Ashford, England: Headley Brothers, 1977), pp. 1–11. Michael S. Moore, *Law and Psychiatry: Rethinking the Relationship* (Cambridge, MA: Cambridge University Press, 1984), pp. 218–19. Abraham Goldstein *The Insanity Defense* (New Haven: Yale University Press, 1967), p. 9ff. See also Richard Moran, *Knowing Right from Wrong: The Insanity Defense of Daniel McNaughton* (New York: The Free Press, 1981).

32. Regina v. Oxford, F. A. Carrington and J. Payne, eds., *Reports of Cases Argued at Nisi Prius*, 9 vols. (London: Sweet, 1825–1891), vol. 9, no. 525, pp. 942–52.

33. Regina v. McNaughton, Howell, ed., *State Trials*, (New Series, 1843), vol. 4, p. 847.

34. H. R. Rollin, "McNaughton's Madness," in West and Walk, eds., *McNaughton*, p. 91.

35. Walker, *Crime and Insanity*, pp. 95–96. Extensive excerpts from the trial,

from the debate in the House of Lords, and the McNaughton Rules are in West and Walk, *McNaughton*, pp. 11–85.

36. *The Times* (London), March 6, 1843, p. 4.

37. West and Walk, *McNaughton*, pp. 11–85.

38. Platt and Diamond, "Origins of the 'Right and Wrong' Test," p. 1,257.

39. 48 Mass. 500 (1844).

40. People v. Coffman, 24 Cal. 230 (1864).

41. State v. Jones, 50 New Hampshire 369 (1871).

42. Fredric Wertham, *The Show of Violence* (New York: Doubleday, 1949), pp. 70–94.

43. Fingarette, *The Meaning of Criminal Insanity*, pp. 175–79.

44. Allen Peskin, *Garfield: A Biography* (Kent, OH: Kent State University Press, 1978), p. 592.

45. Charles E. Rosenberg, *The Trial of the Assassin Guiteau: Psychiatry and Law in the Gilded Age* (Chicago: University of Chicago Press, 1968), p. 89.

46. Davis v. U.S., 160 U.S. 469 (1895).

47. Durham v. U.S., 94 US App. D.C. 228, 45 ALR 2d 1430 (1954).

48. United States v. Brawner, 471 F. 2d. 969 (D.C. Cir. 1972). See Michael S. Moore, *Law and Psychiatry: Rethinking the Relationships* (Cambridge, MA: Cambridge University Press, 1984), pp. 228–32.

49. Herbert Fingarette and Ann Fingarette Hasse, *Disabilities and Criminal Responsibility* (Berkeley: University of California Press, 1979), pp. 117–33.

50. State v. McGee, 361 MO 309, 234 S.W. 2nd 587 (1950).

51. Winslade and Ross, *The Insanity Plea*, p. 26. "Dan White, Killer of San Francisco Mayor, a Suicide," *New York Times*, October 22, 1985, p. A18.

52. Biographical sketch in Caplan, *The Insanity Defense and Hinckley*, pp. 33–47.

53. Ibid., p. 60.

54. Ibid., p. 12.

55. United States v. John W. Hinckley, Jr., 672 F 2d. 115 (D.C. Cir. 1982).

56. American Law Institute, Model Penal Code, 4.01, Proposed Official Draft, 1962. See also Moore, *Law and Psychiatry*, pp. 219–22.

57. *Washington Post*, June 19, 1982, pp. A1, A6; June 22, p. A1, A12.

58. Caplan, *The Insanity Defense and the Trial of John W. Hinckley, Jr.*, pp. 70, 88–89.

59. Ibid., p. 101.

60. "Legal Insanity: Gone Bonkers," *Washington Post*, June 20, 1982, pp. C1 and C5.

61. "Hearings before the Subcommittee on Criminal Law of the Committee on the Judiciary, United States Senate, Ninety-Seventh Congress, Second Session," June 24, 30 and July 14, 1982 (Washington, DC: U.S. Government Printing Office, 1983).

62. *Washington Post*, June 22, 1982, p. A1.

63. "Hearings before the Subcommittee on Criminal Law," p. 160.

64. Comprehensive Crime Control Act of 1984, Public Law 98473, Chapter 313. See American Bar Association, *Report on Standings for Criminal Justice: Nonresponsibility for Crime* (Chicago: American Bar Association, 1983), and American

Psychiatric Association, *Statement of the Insanity Defense* (Washington, DC: American Psychiatric Association, 1982).

65. "Hearings before the Subcommittee on Criminal Law," p. 189.

66. Jones v. United States, 463 U.S. 354 (1982).

67. Norval Morris, "Insanity Defense: The National Institute of Justice Crime File Study Guide" (Washington, DC: U.S. Department of Justice, 1988). See also Rita J. Simon and David E. Aaronson, *The Insanity Defense: A Critical Assessment of Law and Policy in the Post-Hinckley Era* (New York: Praeger, 1988), pp. 8–9.

English Constitutional Documents and Punishment in American Law

Legislators and judges often face the age-old question, "Does the punishment fit the crime?" They are sometimes urged to set up strict penalties to revenge society against notorious offenders, justifying such with the argument that severe punishment will deter similar offenses in the future. Efforts to balance the morality and efficacy of extreme penalties against societal demands for law and order are evident throughout English and American legal thought. The thirteenth-century's Magna Carta in England, the seventeenth-century's English Bill of Rights, and the eighteenth-century's American Bill of Rights all attempted to limit the scope and nature of the state's power to punish wrongdoing. After the constitution makers and legislators attempted to set standards, English and American judges were called on to evaluate the fit of punishment to crime. Questions about inherently cruel penalties, excessive punishments, and sentences not proportional to the crimes committed thus found their way into courtrooms as well as legislative halls. Two landmark cases, England's *Titus Oates* case of 1685[1] and America's *Helm*[2] case of 1983 highlight these questions and illustrate the approaches taken by courts in dealing with crime and its punishment.

FROM TITUS OATES TO JERRY HELM: TWO CASE STUDIES

On May 16, 1685, Titus Oates was brought from prison to the Court of King's Bench to hear sentence pronounced. Convicted of perjury by a London jury, Oates stood before the court condemned for lies which had resulted in barbaric executions of numerous innocent men. The principal inventor of the so-called "Popish Plot" (a nonexistent plot of Catholic priests to assassinate England's King Charles II), Oates had helped to keep England in a state of panic and vindictive rage from 1678 to 1685. Without question Titus Oates was, as described by one judge, "the blackest and most perjured villain that ever appeared upon the face of the earth." Yet as sentence was pronounced against him that day he himself became the object of punishment which would later be called "cruel and unusual."

As Justice Withins of the Court of King's Bench pronounced sentence, he noted that Oates's crimes were so great that it was impossible to find a "proportionable" punishment. English statutory law had reduced the penalties for perjury, Oates's offense. No longer could courts impose the death penalty or tongue mutilation. Under these statutory limitations the court tried to devise a penalty proportionate to Oates's crimes. The sentence was fivefold: First, Oates was to lose his status as clergy; second, he was to be imprisoned for life; third, he was to pay a heavy fine; fourth, he was to be whipped through the streets of London; fifth, he was to stand in the pillory immediately and again on five different dates every year for the remainder of his life.[3]

In the space of four years prominent Englishmen would protest this sentence. In the House of Commons and among some peers in the House of Lords, opinion would focus on the newly enacted English Bill of Rights of 1689 with its provision against cruel and unusual punishments. Some members of the English Parliament of that time would insist that the sentence imposed on Oates violated that clause. Ultimately, this view would prevail and Oates would be set free.[4] The *Oates* case thus gave rise to one of the earliest debates about the meaning of the cruel and unusual punishment clause which was both part of the 1689 English Bill of Rights and later included in the Eighth Amendment to the U.S. Constitution.

Nearly 300 years later the U.S. Supreme Court agreed in 1983 to decide if life imprisonment without parole was an excessive penalty for a six-time offender who had cashed a "no account" check for $100. Mr. Jerry Helm[5] had been convicted by the state of South Dakota of six nonviolent felonies. In 1964, 1966, and 1969 he had been convicted of third-degree burglary. Between 1972 and 1975 he was convicted of obtaining money under false pretenses, of grand larceny, and of a third "driving while intoxicated" offense. Helm's seventh felony offense occurred in 1979. He wrote a check for $100 on a financial institution where he did not have an account. Ordinarily the maximum punishment for this offense would have been five years imprisonment in the state penitentiary and a $5,000 fine. However, because of his criminal record, Jerry Helm was subject to South Dakota's habitual offender law. The

South Dakota Circuit Court, acting under this law, sentenced Helm to life imprisonment without parole because, as the judge said:

I think you certainly earned this sentence and certainly proved that you're an habitual criminal and the record would indicate that you're beyond rehabilitation and that the only prudent thing to do is lock you up for the rest of your natural life, so you won't have further victims of your crimes, just be coming back before Courts. You'll have plenty of time to think this one over.[6]

The question which then went to the U.S. Supreme Court was whether this punishment was excessive or not. Unlike the English justices in *Titus Oates* in 1685, the American Supreme Court justices in *Helm* believed that the sentence imposed by the South Dakota Court was indeed excessive. Their holding stated:

The Constitution requires us to examine Helm's sentence to determine if it is proportionate to his crime. Applying objective criteria, we find that Helm has received the penultimate sentence for relatively minor criminal conduct. He has been treated more harshly than other criminals in the state who have committed more serious crimes. He has been treated more harshly than he would have been in any other jurisdiction, with the possible exception of a single state. We conclude that his sentence is significantly disproportionate to his crime, and is therefore prohibited by the Eighth Amendment.[7]

Jerry Helm was not the villain that Titus Oates was. Oates's false accusations had sent innocent people to their deaths while Helm's crimes were "nonviolent." The linkage between the two cases involved the type of penalty imposed for the crimes and the question of whether the punishment was cruel, unusual, or disproportionate to the crimes committed. The two cases both raised questions about the scope and meaning of the punishment prohibition in the English Bill of Rights of 1689 and its American counterpart, the Eighth Amendment. Between the two cases three centuries elapsed during which legal and moral questions, still discussed today, were debated. In general these issues have been of four kinds: specific "cruel" punishments prohibited under the two documents; "unusual" punishments which should not be inflicted; proportional punishments; and the role of judges in determining sentences. The English legal and historical developments both before and after the case of *Titus Oates* influenced the framers of the U.S. Constitution's Bill of Rights and the decisions of American Courts: the overturning of Jerry Helm's life imprisonment sentence can be better understood within the context of *Titus Oates* and its progeny.

ENGLISH THEORY AND PRACTICE: THE DEVELOPMENT OF THE ENGLISH CRUEL AND UNUSUAL PUNISHMENT PROHIBITION, 900s–1700s

Questions about appropriate punishment for crimes had been raised long before the sentencing of Titus Oates in 1685. English criminal law, a combination of judge-made laws and legislative enactments, constantly struggled to define crimes and impose penalties. For centuries, the English criminal law remained excessively severe in substance. Later, the development of the great documents of Magna Carta (1215), the Petition of Right (1628), and the Bill of Rights (1689) combined to establish individual procedural rights. The dichotomy between a severe, substantive criminal law and the lenient procedural guarantees to life, liberty, and property was basic to the question of determining punishments for crimes.[8] The English response was marked by several distinct periods that offer historical data for understanding the cruel and unusual punishment doctrine.

The most primitive means of punishing offenders in Anglo-Saxon England in the days before King Alfred was by private feuds between the families or clans of the parties involved. It may well have been to limit the excesses and cruelties of these private wars—as well as to assert their own power—that Anglo-Saxon kings developed catalogues of crimes and their appropriate penalties. In their "dooms" or laws Anglo-Saxon kings drew up elaborate and detailed lists of offenses and money fines to be paid as punishment.[9] These early lists often included a scale of liability for damage done to various parts of the body. Monetary values were assigned for the loss of the eye, the ear, the hand, and so on. As in other ancient law codes the penalties were not only proportioned to the gravity of the offense, but also to the status of the victim. However, the local "wise men" of the community, acting as judges, exercised discretion in defining the nature of the crime and the type of punishment. The idea of proportionality and non-excessiveness seemed to be the goal: let the punishment fit the crime.

The Norman Conquest of 1066 set in motion changes in this ancient Anglo-Saxon method of determining penalties. Under William the Conqueror there was a gradual demise of the old fine lists of the Anglo-Saxon kings. The Normans allowed their officials to impose fines and penalties that were often arbitrary and excessive. In addition, William devised unusual punishments to suit his needs. The Norman kings and their officials, however, were under the general restraints of the developing common law. Kings took oaths to "do justice," which included observing legal standards when imposing punishments.[10]

That the old standards rooted in Anglo-Saxon traditions could bind even Norman conquerors became evident in 1215 when King John's excessive fines and cruel treatment of those who opposed him led down the road to Runnymede[11] and Magna Carta. Considered by Englishmen and Americans alike as the basic guarantee of individual rights, Magna Carta provided that no freeman, merchant, clergyman, or lord should be fined except "according to the magnitude of the delinquency." Magna Carta's Article 20 became a major barrier to coercive state power and valuable precedent which judges and legislators used in the following centuries to restrict excessive penalties. Severe physical punishments were also debated in a document alleged to date from the time of King Edward I. The specific provision relating to excessive physical punishment read as follows:

We do forbid that a person shall be condemned to death for a trifling offense. But for the correction of the multitude, extreme punishment shall be inflicted according to the nature and extent of the offense.[12]

The Tudor-Stuart epoch (1480s–1680s) created the immediate setting for the American understanding of cruel and unusual punishments. The Tudor monarchs—Henry VII, Henry VIII, Edward VI, Mary, and Elizabeth I—all had to cope with political unrest and widespread lawlessness. Such circumstances provoked severe, harsh punishments to preserve law and order. These included burning at the stake; drowning, hanging, and quartering; whipping, branding, and mutilation. The very worst punishments were reserved for traitors and heretics; however, any offense designated a "felony" could also carry a severe penalty. The list of felonies grew longer each year. Crimes like robbery, arson, and rape carried the death penalty of hanging and often had the super-added punishment of quartering. Fearing violent overthrow of government, the Tudors resorted frequently to Star Chamber, a special court. This body, not hindered by ordinary legal procedures, could act swiftly and efficiently to enforce the royal will and prevent disorder. Star Chamber's favorite penalties were enormous fines for the rich and it increasingly developed a taste for severe corporal punishments for poor offenders. When Star Chamber was finally abolished by Parliament in 1641, it had come to symbolize excessiveness in punishments.[13]

The Stuart kings—James I, Charles I, Charles II, and James II—also used cruel and unusual punishment to deter their enemies. The Petition of Right of 1628 protesting such sentences, expressly forbade punishment of civilians by King Charles I's military courts. The king was forced to accept the Petition, but he consistently worked to evade it.[14] Even after the turbulent era of the English Civil War, Stuart kings and their judges still possessed the means to punish those who displeased them. The practice of inflicting cruel punishments continued during the period following the restoration under Charles II in 1660: it was out of this setting that the *Titus Oates* case emerged.

Titus Oates, an adventurer of uncertain background, had apparently concluded that crisis could produce opportunities for enhancing one's fame and fortune. He manipulated some information about a meeting of English Jesuits to create a national emergency which became known as the "Popish Plot." Oates accused five Catholic noblemen of plotting to assassinate the king. He claimed that he had seen the commission issued to them by the pope. Moreover, Oates added even more victims to his list of participants: All were convicted and put to death for complicity in this imaginary plot. Their executions followed the barbarous custom described by the highest judges of England in passing sentence on Richard Langhorn and five companions for their supposed complicity in the plot:

That you be . . . drawn to the place of execution upon hurdles; That you be then severally hanged by the neck; That you be cut down alive; That your privy members be cut off; That your bowels be taken out and burned in your view. That your heads be severed from your bodies; That your bodies be divided into four quarters.[15]

Cruel punishments continued during James II's infamous "Bloody Assizes" of 1686. Drawing, hanging disemboweling, and quartering became a usual sentence; extended whippings were also allowed, often resulting in death. James II's chief justice, George Jeffreys, aggressively used his power under a special royal commission to pile punishment on top of punishment. He thus created "unusual" punishments for offenders. It was he who presided at the trial of Titus Oates and joined in imposing the bizarre and cruel penalty on Oates.

Was Oates's punishment within the law? The judges believed that the end justified the means and took advantage of the fact that the law had not set a limit on the amount of ordinary penalties that could be collectively imposed. Nevertheless, the question arose even then: "Was Oates's penalty, if legal, unusually cruel?" Reaction to the barbaric and excessive penalties imposed upon those convicted at Jeffreys' Bloody Assizes and upon Titus Oates soon helped shake the very foundations of the Stuart monarchy.

Out of this struggle for power emerged the English Bill of Rights, giving specific formulation to the principle that excessive penalties and cruel and unusual punishments should be prohibited. As the members of Parliament struggled to articulate the rights and privileges that the new monarchs, William and Mary, would be required to guarantee, they focused attention particularly on the penalties imposed on Oates. During the parliamentary debates, terms like "cruel," "barbarous," "inhuman," "unchristian," and "illegal" were all used to describe Oates's sentence. Many believed that such punishments would, in the future, be prohibited under the Bill of Rights. The practice of increasing "usual" penalties like whipping and pillorying until they became excessive was criticized as "unusual." Thus by 1689 the concept that cruel and unusual punishments should be prohibited was formalized in English constitutional law.[16]

Clearly, the concept itself has evolved. It had emerged in the Anglo-Saxon period as a principle of proportionality and non-excessiveness of penalties and had found a place in Magna Carta. It grew and matured in the crucible of the Popish Plot and the events of the Bloody Assizes. By 1689 Englishmen were inspired to combine their ancient traditions, the experiences of past historical events, and the contemporary examples of the punishment of Titus Oates into a maxim that would prohibit cruel and unusual punishments. Americans in turn would draw upon all of these English experiences to write the Eighth Amendment to the U.S. Constitution.

THE AMERICAN CRUEL AND UNUSUAL PUNISHMENT PROHIBITION

The barbarous punishments known and practiced in England also appeared in colonial America, but American colonists demonstrated quite early that they did not approve of "cruel and unusual punishments." The 1641 "Body of Liberties" of Massachusetts contained no less than six articles prohibiting torture, brutality, and cruel punishment. At the onset of the American Revolution eight of the thirteen colonies included prohibitions against cruel and unusual punishment in their state constitutions. The wording varied somewhat from state to state, with several states combining both theories of proportionality and prohibition of certain methods.[17]

It was the Virginia Declaration of Rights (1776), using the exact phrase of the 1689 English Bill of Rights, that most directly influenced other states. The Virginia provisions stated: "That excessive bail ought not be required, nor excessive fines imposed, nor cruel and unusual punishments inflicted."[18] George Mason, a delegate to the Virginia Convention in 1776, submitted this resolution. A recognized colonial authority on English constitutional history and law, Mason was familiar with the English constitutional documents and the works of English legal authorities such as Hale and Blackstone. Although Hale's writings had not emphasized the issue of cruel and unusual punishments, Blackstone had provided an extensive discussion of torture and of excessive fines, imprisonments, and punishments. Blackstone noted that an atrocious crime required a "super-added" penalty to that of death. He recognized hanging as the usual method of execution with "drawing," "embowelling alive," beheading, and quartering added for especially heinous crimes. For noncapital crimes Blackstone listed a number of penalties: mutilation, whipping, and the use of the pillory and stocks. Banishment, imprisonment, fines, or loss of civil and political rights were also included. Judges had power to determine fines and imprisonment for noncapital crimes. Blackstone declared that the English Bill of Rights of 1689 prohibited penalties like those imposed in "some unprecedented proceedings in the Court of King's Bench, in the reign of King James the Second." This referred to the penalties and punishments imposed on Titus Oates. Colonists like George Mason had studied Blackstone's *Commentaries* carefully. They also knew their English history including the penalties imposed by Star Chamber, by the Bloody Assizes, and by judges in the trial of Titus Oates.[19]

However, the cruel and unusual punishments' prohibition was not part of the original seven articles of the Constitution of the United States. The majority of the delegates who assembled in Philadelphia believed that the power divisions and limitations on government were sufficient to protect individual rights, although some delegates, like Virginia's Richard Lee, urged inclusion of a specific provision dealing with prohibited punishments. Lee's view was later echoed in several of the state-ratifying conventions. One Massachusetts delegate, a Mr. Holmes, expressed concern because, as he said, the Constitution did not restrain Congress "from inventing the most cruel and unheard of punishments and annexing them to crimes . . . racks and gibbets may be amongst the most mild instruments of their discipline." In Virginia, Patrick Henry repeated the fear that unless Congress were specifically prohibited from imposing "excessive fines and bail" and from "inflicting cruel and unusual punishments" it might adopt the customs of civil law countries like Germany, France, and Spain.[20]

Such concerns led quickly to the adoption of the Eighth Amendment to the U.S. Constitution. Proposed by James Madison in the House of Representatives of the First Congress, this article forbidding cruel and unusual punishments was opposed by only two delegates. Mr. Smith of South Carolina objected to the words "nor cruel and unusual punishments." It was his opinion that "the impact of them [is] too indefinite." Mr. Livermore from New Hampshire noted that the only way a definition of excessive bail or excessive fines could be determined would be by courts and judges. He then specifically indicated why he was unhappy with the "nor cruel and unusual punishments" clause. His argument went as follows:

No cruel and unusual punishment is to be inflicted; it is sometimes necessary to hang a man, villains often deserve whipping, and perhaps having their ears cut off; but are we in future to be prevented from inflicting these punishments because they are cruel? If a more lenient mode of correcting vice and deterring others from the commission of it could be invented, it would be very prudent in the legislature to adopt it; but until we have some security that this will be done, we ought not to be restrained from making necessary laws by any declaration of this kind.[21]

There is no record of any one debating with Livermore concerning his interpretation of the clause. No one insisted that the punishments mentioned were not touched by the clause. The House adopted the proposal and sent it to the Senate. Only minor changes occurred here and the cruel and unusual punishment clause retained its form: the Bill of Rights with its punishment limitation came into force on December 15, 1791.

The scope of the Eighth Amendment became a major concern during the Reconstruction Period following the American Civil War. During debate on the Fourteenth Amendment, several congressmen wanted to impose limits on states where "cruel and unusual punishments have been inflicted under state laws."[22] However, it required a series of Supreme Court decisions before state actions involving excessive punishments could be prohibited under the Eighth Amendment. Finally, using the Fourteenth Amendment, the Court in 1962 in *Robinson v. California,* 370 U.S. 660 specifically held that state laws inflicting cruel and unusual punishments were unconstitutional. Questions about prohibited punishments moved with greater frequency into courts and they, as well as the legislators, thus became crucial decision makers.

JUDGES AND PUNISHMENTS: ENGLAND AND AMERICA

The *Titus Oates* case raised questions about punishments that were prohibited because they were cruel and unusual or disproportionate; it also dramatized the role of the judge in determining penalties and defining terms. English judges had always believed themselves to be uniquely qualified to draw lines between levels of punishments. They exercised broad discretionary power to develop procedures and legal actions by which a person could be prosecuted, convicted, and sentenced. Even before Magna Carta, English judges were responsible for enunciating the law. Sometimes this was no more than a judicial statement of the tradition and norms of a community, an articulation of a longstanding practice. Sometimes it was an interpretation of a written statute or law.[23] Judges, not legislators, devised the test of "malice aforethought" to differentiate murder from other homicide. Again, judges acted to separate petit or trial juries from grand or presentment juries and to require, by 1367, a unanimous verdict in a jury trial. English judges invented the writ of habeas corpus centuries before the English Parliament perfected it by statute in 1679 and the U.S. Constitution reaffirmed it in 1787. Judges set limits to arbitrary imprisonments.[24]

In three early English court cases involving punishment and penalties judges claimed power to determine the appropriateness of the sentence. In a 1316 case,[25] judges questioned whether a fine of two horses was excessive. The court ordered the bailiff of the bishop of Winchester to stand trial to determine if, in seizing this property, he had violated the Magna Carta. In the 1615 case of *Hodges v. Humkin*[26] the court issued a writ of habeas corpus upon the mayor of Liskerret. This official had thrown Hodges into a dungeon, starved him, and denied him an appeal. Hodges's crime was "undecent language, spitting, and evil gestures." The court, claiming power to "judge of the sufficiency" of the crime and its penalty proceeded to set standards. These included: proper procedures; a legal right to inflict such a punishment; the nature of the punishment; and whether the punishment was proportional to the crime committed.[27] In the *Titus Oates* case the judges discussed in detail judicial power and authority as well as jurisdiction.[28] They claimed that Parliament had given "discretion to the court to inflict such punishment as they [the judges] think fit; yet not heavier than the crimes deserved."[29]

American judges followed English tradition in asserting judicial authority to evaluate punishments and to develop standards and guidelines for identifying cruel and unusual punishments. They developed at least eight tests that have proved highly significant over time. These included: (1) the historical practices standard for defining a cruel punishment; (2) the statutory provision test; (3) the test of legislative intent and purpose; (4) the test for valid legislative power; (5) the "evolving standards of decency" test; (6) the "shocking to the conscience" test; (7) the "due process" test; (8) the excessiveness or disproportionality test. Each of these standards drew upon English constitutional documents and judicial practices for their understanding and application.

The test for prohibited historical practices focused on the method of inflicting punishment. The U. S. Supreme Court in *Wilkerson v. Utah*, in 1879, referred to the fourth volume of Blackstone's *Commentaries* and held, "that punishments of torture, such as those mentioned [by Blackstone], and all others in the same line of unnecessary cruelty, are forbidden by [the Eighth] Amendment to the Constitution."[30] The Court later expanded it to include burning at the stake, crucifixion, and breaking on the wheel. Such were prohibited by the Constitution because they involved lingering death rather than mere extinguishment of life.[31] Barbaric methods of punishments including the rack, the thumbscrew, and the iron boot, were likewise outlawed.[32] Death itself as a penalty was not, however, defined historically as being either cruel or unusual.

U.S. courts also followed English judicial requirements that legislative statutes identify penalties. English judges at the time of the *Titus Oates* case noted that Parliament had by statute limited the punishment for perjury so that mutilation and death could not be imposed. Englishmen came therefore to believe that absent a specific statutory authorization for imposing a life sentence, not even judges could prescribe such a penalty. Supporters of Titus Oates, protesting his sentence, also pointed out that Parliament had not authorized life imprisonment for a perjury conviction. Statutory definition of a penalty was thus historically significant in English practice.[33] U.S. courts expected American law makers to follow this approach. Legislators were expected to include in the written laws specific mention of the penalty to be imposed. The case of *In re Medley,* 134 U.S. 160 (1889) held that solitary confinement was an "additional" punishment. As such, it could not be levied on a condemned murderer in America unless provided for by statute.

The test of legislative intent, motive, and purpose allowed courts to expand judicial powers. Attempting to determine the intent of the Magna Carta was a traditional approach of English judges. Was not the intent of the Magna Carta the limitation of excessive fines and exemption of certain possessions from forfeit? Litigants often pressed this point, as did Richard Le Gras in the case of his horses. American judges also believed that it was necessary to look for legislative intent, motive, and purpose in written law: they set up guidelines and standards to determine legislative intent. Some legislative bodies would define the intent of a statute's penalty to be deterrence of crime and protection of society. Courts might then test this penalty. Thus, when state legislatures established sterilization as a penalty, courts inquired whether this was punishment or something else. If the penalty actually would protect society and provide for the general welfare, it might be legal. If, however, it showed passion and prejudice on the part of the legislature, it could be struck down as violation of the prohibition against cruel and unusual punishments. This court-imposed test in *Skinner v. State of Oklahoma ex rel Williamson*, 316 U.S. 535(1942) finally ended sterilization for those deemed to possess criminal traits.

Courts also tested the authority of legislative bodies to impose a particular sentence. In England, Parliament, the legislative body, was supreme and held power unlimited by courts. According to English lawyers, "It is a fundamental principle . . . that Parliament can do everything but make a woman a man, and a man a woman."[34] Blackstone said, "What the Parliament doth, no authority upon earth can undo." In short, Parliament could do everything that was not naturally impossible.[35] Nevertheless, other documents such as *Confirmatio Cartarum* of 1297 and the *Tallagis non Concedendo* of 1306 had set up Magna Carta as "higher law" and asserted that statutes or judgments contrary to Magna Carta should be "undone and holden for nought." One prominent English judge claimed the right to declare acts of Parliament unconstitutional based on the common law traditions of the realm. Thus in *Bonham's Case* (1609) Coke, in dictum, stated

The common law will control acts of parliament, and sometimes adjudge them to be utterly void; for when an act of parliament is against common right and reason, or repugnant, or impossible to be performed, the common law will control it, and adjudge such act to be void.[36]

Although Englishmen ignored Coke's dictum, Americans adopted and extended it. The U. S. Constitution took the place of Magna Carta and Congress was denied power to enact laws repugnant to the provisions of the Constitution. The guarantees of the Bill of Rights as well as the prohibitions against *ex post facto* laws and bills of attainder placed limits on Congress. Courts used these constitutional standards to hold Congress accountable; legislative punishments had to be constitutional.

Another significant standard set by American courts to test sentences became known as the "evolving standards of decency" test. The justices in the *Titus Oates* case had recognized evolving standards. Mutilation and death for a perjury conviction had been abolished by statute law. The justices explained the evolving standards by recalling:

It is known that by the old laws of England perjury was punished with death; it grew a little more moderate afterwards, not to make the crime the less, but because of the danger there might be of malice.... But the next step was cutting out of the tongue...[thus] punish[ing] that impious crime of perjury with the most terrible punishments. Since that time our ancestors have yet been more moderate, and have not extended the judgment to life and member.[37]

The evolving standards of decency test became central in U.S. death penalty cases. Beginning with *Furman v. Georgia,* 408 U.S. 238 (1972) and continuing with *Gregg v. Georgia, 428 U.S. 153 (1976), Coker v. Georgia,* 433 U.S. 584 (1977), and *Enmund v. Florida,* 458 U.S. 782 (1982) the U.S. Supreme Court compared state laws to identify evolving standards. In 1989, in a series of death penalty cases involving juveniles and the mentally retarded, the Court defined the evolving standards of decency test thus:

In determining whether a punishment violates evolving standards of decency, this court looks not to its own subjective conceptions, but, rather, to the conceptions of modern American society as reflected by objective evidence.... The primary and most reliable evidence of national consensus—the pattern of federal and state laws—fails to [show] a settled consensus against the execution of 16- and 17-year-old offenders. Of the 37 states that permit capital punishment, 15 decline to impose it on 16-year-olds and 12 on 17-year-olds. This does not establish the degree of national agreement this Court has previously thought sufficient to label a punishment cruel and unusual.[38]

The justices also linked proportionality analysis and the evolving standards of decency test together to hold that "proportionality analysis itself can only be conducted on the basis of the [evolving] standards [of decency]."[39]

A "shocking to the conscience" test developed alongside the evolving standards of decency test. English justices in the *Hodges* case in 1615 were shocked by the "very barbarous" and "malicious" penalty inflicted for disorderly behavior. One justice expressed horror that the defendant had been "imprisoned . . . in a dungeon, without bed, bread, or meat . . . without any just cause at all."[40] American judges in state and federal courts would also make the shocking nature of a punishment grounds for prohibition as, for example, in the 1910 case of *Weems v. United States*.[41]

Another standard used in defining prohibited punishments is the "due process of law" test. Due process of law, a fundamental right of Englishmen, was brought from the Mother Country by the earliest settlers and established in the colonies. It was a part of ancient Anglo-Saxon institutions, a central feature of both Magna Carta, and the 1689 English Bill of Rights. Coke's statements on the meaning of due process of law exercised a critical influence in America. As a leader in the House of Commons and former chief justice, Coke protested the arbitrary actions of King Charles I and helped formulate the 1628 Petition of Right. Thus Parliament reaffirmed the ancient concept of due process of law. It would be repeated again and again in the American colonies.[42] Its precise meaning, however, remained open. American courts early identified due process as "those settled usages and modes of proceedings existing in the common and statute laws of England before the emigration of our ancestors. . . . The words 'due process of law' were undoubtedly intended to convey the same meaning as the words 'by the law of the land' in *Magna Carta*."[43] What did this mean when the question of punishments arose? In *McGautha v. California*, 402 U.S. 350(1971) the defendant claimed that it was a violation of due process for the same jury that had determined his guilt to also determine the impact of insanity on his sentence. Would a death penalty be cruel and unusual under those circumstances? Justice Harlan and the Court majority found no violation of due process or the cruel and unusual punishment prohibition. The justices in the minority, using other English legal and historical data, did.

Balancing the nature of the crime against the penalty imposed is another approach to the cruel and unusual punishment prohibition. Often referred to as the proportionality standard, this test asks the question,

"Does the punishment fit the crime?" It goes to the heart of the Eighth Amendment and has occupied the attention of jurists and legal scholars from early times. Does the prohibition apply only to the methods or modes of inflicting punishment, or does it prohibit "excessive" penalties? In answering this question, American judges turned to English constitutional documents and to case precedents for answers. Two significant English case examples, already discussed, have been used by courts: *Le Gras v. Bailiff of the Bishop of Winchester* (1316) and *Hodges v. Humkin* (1615). The first case decision found a fine of two horses to be excessive; the second overturned an indefinite confinement sentence as not proportionate. An additional case known as the *Earl of Devon's Case* (1689)[44] identified an excessive fine in a personal assault case as cruel and unusual.

The theory that excessive or disproportionate sentences were prohibited by the cruel and unusual punishment limitation in the U.S. Bill of Rights appeared in numerous early American court cases. Attorneys argued as a matter of course that excessive degrees of punishment were prohibited by the Constitution. American courts, like their English counterparts, arrived at decisions on a case by case basis. They considered the nature of the crime and the defendant as they tested for excessiveness. For instance, the crime of rape, long recognized as one of the most heinous crimes, carried the death penalty in earlier times. Yet, in *Coker v. Georgia*, 433 U.S. 584 (1977) the U. S. Supreme Court invalidated the death penalty for rape of an *adult* woman. The crime of armed robbery in which death occurs has also long been considered a heinous crime and carried the death penalty in many states. However, in 1982 in *Enmund v. Florida*, 458 U.S. 782, the Supreme Court found that the extension of the death penalty to a *participant* in such a crime—one who had not himself taken life—was excessive.

Courts have also tested for excessive punishment in cases where the sentence—although severe—was not a death penalty. These cases have included issues such as sodomy, selling illegal and harmful substances, forgery and passing bad checks. In each case judicial standards determined if the punishment imposed was proportional to the crime itself. Thus in the 1892 landmark case of *O'Neil v. State of Vermont*, the U.S. Supreme Court evaluated the penalties imposed for selling illegal substances. John O'Neill had been found guilty of 307 separate offenses involving the unlicensed selling of liquor transported from New York to Vermont. O'Neil's fine was set at $6,638.72 or twenty dollars per offense plus court costs. If O'Neil failed to pay his fine within the deadline, he would be sentenced to fifty-four years at hard labor: three days per dollar as provided by Vermont law. Was the penalty excessive? The majority of justices in the case did not answer, deciding the issues on procedural grounds. However, three justices in dissent did find the penalty excessive: it was six times as great as could have been imposed for manslaughter, forgery or perjury. Justices Field, Harlan, and Brewer interpreted the Eighth Amendment to outlaw not only cruel and unusual punishment, but those which were excessive. They wrote:

The inhibition [of the Eighth Amendment] is directed . . . against all punishments which by their excessive length or severity are greatly disproportioned to the offenses charged. The whole inhibition is against that which is excessive either in the bail required, or fine imposed, or punishments inflicted. . . . It does not alter its character as cruel and unusual, that for each distinct offense there is a small punishment, if, when they are brought together and one punishment for the whole is inflicted, it becomes one of excessive severity.[45]

The question of whether the death penalty could be imposed on drug dealers was raised following the passage of the Federal Anti-Drug Abuse Act of 1988. This statute provided capital punishment for certain drug-related offenses; states also enacted similar laws. The Supreme Court's only limitation on the death penalty was "an individualized assessment of [its] appropriateness." This was stated in *Jurek v. Texas,* 428 U.S. 262 (1976).

COMBINING TESTS: THE U.S. SUPREME COURT AT WORK

As U.S. courts developed these various standards for interpreting the Eighth Amendment, different views appeared among the justices based on their approach to English and American constitutional documents and legal history. Some thought the historical standards test alone should define cruel and unusual punishment; others stressed the disproportionate penalty concept; still others believed that evolving standards of decency should define cruel and unusual punishment. Differing interpretations within each test also emerged. Several landmark cases demonstrate these judicial struggles to give final and certain meaning to the Eighth Amendment.

One of the earliest cases in which the legal history of the cruel and unusual punishment prohibition was interpreted differently by the justices of the Supreme Court was *Weems v. United States.*[46] English precedents and constitutional documents were analyzed in painstaking detail by the justices in both the majority and in the minority. The *Weems* case raised questions about both cruel and unusual, and disproportionate, penalties. In this forgery case, Paul A. Weems, a disbursing officer of the U.S. Bureau of Coast Guard and Transportation in the Philippine Islands falsified a cash book. He made two entries—one for 208 pesos and one for 408 pesos—which he labelled as wages for some lighthouse employees but never paid to those individuals. Weems was sentenced to fifteen years imprisonment during which time he was to wear a chain at the ankle and wrist, and perform hard and painful labor. He was denied contact with friends or family. When his term of imprisonment ceased he was placed on perpetual parole. He was denied the right to travel without prior approval of his parole officer, and disqualified from holding office or voting.

The justices in the majority in *Weems* focused on the principle of proportionality. In the words of Justice McKenna, "punishment for crime should be graduated and proportional to offense." Weems's punishment according to these justices was "cruel in its excess of imprisonment and that which accompanies and follows imprisonment." Justice McKenna noted that some courts, using the tyrannical acts of the English monarchs and Blackstone's description of superadded penalties, had concluded that "punishment of torture, such as those mentioned [by Blackstone]... and others of unnecessary cruelty [like the Stuarts] are forbidden by [the Eighth] Amendment to the Constitution." He observed, however, that other courts also believed that the cruel and unusual punishment prohibition was directed not only against torture, but against all penalties excessive, severe, and disproportionate to the offenses charged. Adopting this latter view, Justice McKenna held that the American cruel and unusual punishment prohibition went beyond preventing acts like those of Stuart monarchs in England. McKenna was convinced that the framers of the Eighth Amendment knew that "there could be exercise of cruelty by laws other than those which inflicted bodily pain or mutilation and wanted to limit the legislative power to "fix terms of imprisonment with what[ever] accompaniments they might [choose]."

Moreover, Justice McKenna also believed that if the English Bill of Rights had been designed to prevent disproportionate punishments as opposed to merely torturous methods, then it would follow that the Eighth Amendment of the American Constitution should do likewise. Was the English Bill of Rights "not intended to warn against merely erratic modes of punishment or torture, but applied expressly to 'bail', 'fines', and 'punishments' "? McKenna's analysis of the *Earl of Devon's* case (1689) revealed that Englishmen had interpreted the prohibition to forbid an excessive fine in a simple assault and battery action. For Justice McKenna and the majority justices in *Weems,* this precedent settled the question of proportionality versus torture. The cruel and unusual punishment prohibition of the American Eighth Amendment, like the English, not only outlawed torture but also required that the punishment be proportional to the crime.

The two justices in the minority disagreed. Yet they too turned to English constitutional documents and legal history to justify their opposition. Writing for himself and for Justice Oliver Wendell Holmes,

Justice Edward White traced the migration of the cruel and unusual punishment doctrine to America. White used English sources that included the trial of Titus Oates in seventeenth-century England; he devoted over five pages of his opinion to a discussion and analysis of the *Oates* case. Here White found the origin and meaning of the cruel and unusual punishment prohibition as it had evolved in England. He first highlighted the penalties that had been imposed upon Titus Oates by the Court of King's Bench: extended whipping, and yearly pillorying, and life imprisonment. While whipping and the pillory were both usual modes of punishment, White observed, the English court had combined them into a new, unusual punishment. In addition, the imposition of a sentence of life imprisonment was very unusual in English law and practice of the 1680s. Only Parliament had power to create such a penalty. Was this the type of penalty which the English framers had in mind when they wrote the English Bill of Rights? Justice White believed that it was. He found proof for this linkage in a House of Commons committee report stating that Oates's sentence was illegal since there were no precedents for whipping and for life imprisonment for perjury. The report also claimed that the sentence imposed on Oates was cruel, barbarous, illegal, and contrary to English law and ancient practice. The report concluded that the sentence imposed upon Oates was "contrary to the declaration [the English Bill of Rights] on the 12th of February last [1689]."

White's study of the parliamentary debates surrounding this report convinced him that Oates's type of punishment was exactly what was meant by "unusual" in the English Bill of Rights. Imposing "customary bodily punishments" cumulatively to create a new type of penalty was prohibited as "unusual." Oates's penalty was also illegal because the penalties of whipping and pillorying had been combined to create a new type of penalty not recognized by law. Additionally, certain penalties could not be imposed by court or crown absent specific parliamentary authorization, and even Parliament could not authorize a return to the inhuman penalties of the past. Thus Titus Oates's sentence to life imprisonment by the Court of King's Bench was invalid since Parliament had not given the court specific statutory power.

From linkage of the *Oates* case to the English Bill of Rights, Justice White found a test for "cruel and unusual." Punishments would be ruled invalid if they were repetitious of the atrocious elements characterizing many executions imposed by English kings and queens. A punishment would also be invalid if a court or executive tried to impose a penalty not prescribed by the legislature in a statute. Combining a number of valid, authorized penalties to create a new punishment was "unusual" and thus illegal. Justice White believed that the American framers of the Eighth Amendment had understood the intent of their English forebears and had likewise intended a similar meaning for their cruel and unusual punishment clause. White concluded that,

It was only intended by [the Eighth] Amendment to remedy the wrongs which had been provided against in the English Bill of Rights; it . . . operate [as] a direct and controlling prohibition upon the legislative branch, restraining it from authorizing . . . the infliction of the cruel bodily punishments of the past, which was one of the evils sought to be prevented for the future by the English Bill of Rights, and also restrained the courts from exerting and Congress from empowering them to select . . . modes of punishment which were not usual, or usual modes of punishment to a degree not usual and which could alone be imposed by express authority of law.[47]

Justice White's textual analysis highlighting the *Oates* case left him with a circumscribed and narrow view of the cruel and unusual punishment prohibition. Legislative bodies were limited only from imposing the type of torturous and barbarous punishments used before 1689—such as drawing, hanging, and quartering. Both Justice McKenna, for the majority, and Justice White, for the minority, had focused on the original intent of the framers of the English Bill of Rights: each had reached a different conclusion.

The relevance of the *Oates* case for understanding the Eighth Amendment to the U.S. Constitution continued to be a critical point in American court decisions. Modern constitutional scholars do agree that this precedent defines the cruel and unusual punishments clause of the 1689 English Bill of Rights to forbid punishments "unauthorized by statute and outside the jurisdiction of the sentencing court."[48] In addition, modern scholars also have used still earlier historical evidence to argue that the English clause reiterated an older tradition against disproportionate punishments. These historical roots influenced the approach adopted by the U.S. Supreme Court in the death penalty case of *Furman v. Georgia* in 1972.[49]

Furman was a consolidation of three different cases, the defendants in each having been sentenced to death for the crime committed. William Furman, a twenty-six year old mentally deficient black, was convicted of the murder of a white householder. Lucius Jackson, a twenty-one year old black was convicted of the rape of a white woman. The third case also involved a borderline mentally deficient black man who had raped a white woman. The supreme courts of Georgia and Texas upheld the convictions and the death sentence; the U.S. Supreme Court reversed because the death penalty had been applied in an arbitrary manner. In the numerous opinions written by the justices in the majority and in the minority, questions about English doctrines and practices were again raised. There were at least three specific questions: (1) What did the English Bill of Rights prohibition of cruel and unusual punishment mean in the minds of Englishmen of that day? (2) What events of English history affected American drafters of the Eighth Amendment? (3) Could an analysis of this data settle the long-debated question as to whether the clause prohibited only certain types of punishments or whether it also prohibited disproportionate penalties?

Justice Thurgood Marshall's opinion made the most extensive use of the legal history of the cruel and unusual punishment prohibition as it developed in English law. Marshall analyzed the English treason trials of 1685—the "Bloody Assizes"—which had spurred the adoption of the English Bill of Rights. He noted that the trial of Titus Oates might have had more influence on the English document than the Bloody Assizes, since many members of Parliament had declared that the punishments imposed on Oates were "unauthorized by statute" and were "disproportionate" penalties. Which event of English history had the greatest impact on the cruel and unusual prohibition clause? Marshall refused to decide. However, he concluded that, at least, inhumane punishments were outlawed. He stated his opinion forcefully:

Whether the English Bill of Rights prohibition against cruel and unusual punishment is properly read as a response to excessive or illegal punishments, or as reaction to barbaric and objectionable modes of punishment, or as both, there is no doubt whatever that in borrowing the language and including it in the Eighth Amendment, our Founding Fathers intended to outlaw torture and other cruel punishments.[50]

Furman did not settle questions about the death penalty and the Eighth Amendment. The Supreme Court continued to confront questions about the cruelty and excessiveness of the death penalty in subsequent cases. In *Gregg v. Georgia,* 428 U. S. 153(1976) the Court refused to find that the Eighth Amendment, standing alone, prohibited the imposition of the death penalty. According to Justice Potter Stewart, history and precedent as well as the text of the Constitution itself showed that the framers did not believe that the sentence of death for the crime of murder was a per se violation of the Eighth and Fourteenth Amendments. In *Coker v. Georgia,* 433 U.S. 584(1977) and *Enmund v. Florida,* 458 U.S. 782(1982) the Court tried to articulate the parameters of the death penalty. In these two cases the Court held that death was an excessive and disproportionate penalty for rape or felony murder if the defendant did not himself commit the murder or intend that lethal force be used. The Court in these cases ascertained the fit of punishment to crime and focused on an examination of the facts peculiar to each case.

The excessiveness of the death penalty for juveniles was raised in 1989 in two cases: *Stanford v. Kentucky,* and *Wilkins v. Missouri.*[51] Kevin Stanford, age seventeen, was convicted of murder, first degree sodomy, first

degree robbery, and receiving stolen property; Heath Wilkins, age sixteen, was convicted of first degree murder, armed criminal action, and
carrying a concealed weapon. Both were sentenced to death. Both asked
the Supreme Court to consider whether imposition of the death penalty
on those who were juveniles when they committed their crimes fell within
the Eighth Amendment's prohibition against cruel and unusual punishment. Since the court had ruled just the year before in *Thompson v.
Oklahoma*,[52] that imposition of the death penalty on juveniles of fifteen
was unconstitutional under proportionality analysis of the Eighth
Amendment, the question in *Stanford v. Kentucky* was that of line drawing.
Would the court extend Thompson to rule that sixteen and seventeen
year-old juveniles were also protected under the Eighth Amendment?
In announcing the judgment of the Court, Justice Antonin Scalia stated
that the death sentences in each case would not have been either a "mode
or act of punishment . . . considered cruel and unusual at the time that
the Bill of Rights was adopted." Quoting Blackstone and Hale, Justice
Scalia pointed out that the "common law set the rebuttable presumption
of incapacity to commit any felony at the age of 14, and theoretically
permitted capital punishment to be imposed on anyone over the age of
7." The standards of this common-law tradition in America had permitted the execution of 281 offenders under the age of eighteen and
126 under the age of seventeen according to Justice Scalia, and, he
concluded, there was no "historical . . . consensus forbidding the imposition of capital punishment on any person who murders at 16 or 17
years of age." Thus such punishment did not "offend the Eighth Amendment's prohibition against cruel and unusual punishment." Moreover,
applying the evolving standards of decency test, Scalia noted that there
was no national consensus expressed in state legislative enactments re-
pudiating the death penalty for sixteen and seventeen-year old juveniles.
Standards had not evolved to identify these as cruel and unusual.

   The question of whether the execution of mentally retarded capital
murderers constituted cruel and unusual punishment was also addressed
by the Supreme Court in 1989. In *Penry v. Lynaugh*[53] the opinion of
Justice O'Connor, concurred in by Chief Justice Rehnquist and Justices
White, Scalia, and Kennedy, rehearsed the historical background of English law. Justice O'Connor reiterated the earlier view expressed in *Ford
v. Wainwright*[54] that punishments considered cruel and unusual at the
time the Bill of Rights was adopted *were* prohibited by the Eighth Amendment. She agreed that the prohibitions of the Eighth Amendment were
not limited "to those practices condemned by the common law in 1789
[when the constitution was adopted]," but recognized the "evolving standards of decency." O'Connor explored the standards of English common
law regarding the mentally retarded in the following passage:

It was well settled at common law that "idiots," together with "lunatics," were not subject to punishment for criminal acts committed under those incapacities. As Blackstone wrote, "...Idiots and lunatics are not chargeable for their own acts, if committed when under those incapacities..." [4 W. Blackstone, Commentaries *24-*25]. See also 1 W. Hawkins, Pleas of the Crown 1–2 (7th ed. 1795), "[T]hose who are under a natural disability of distinguishing between good and evil, as idiots and lunatics, are not punishable by any criminal prosecution whatsoever." Idiocy was understood as "a defect of understanding from the moment of birth," in contrast to lunacy which was "a partial derangement of the intellectual faculties, the senses returning at uncertain intervals."[55]

O'Connor continued her analysis by noting that while there was no one definition of idiocy at common law, the term had generally been used to describe those incapable of distinguishing between good and evil. Quoting from Matthew Hale's *Pleas of the Crown,* and from the 1723 trial of Edward Arnold, O'Connor emphasized the refusal of the common law to execute idiots and lunatics.[56] She then linked the "old common law notion of idiocy to modern mental retardation and turned to the question of punishment of the mentally retarded in the following analysis:

The common law prohibition against punishing "idiots" for their crimes suggests that it may indeed be "cruel and unusual" punishment to execute persons who are profoundly or severely retarded and wholly lacking the capacity to appreciate the wrongfulness of their action.[57]

However, the Court refused to hold that the Eighth Amendment's prohibition of cruel and unusual punishment precluded the execution of *any* mentally retarded person. Instead, the Court held that

so long as sentencers can consider...mitigating evidence of mental retardation in imposing sentence, an individualized determination of whether "death is the appropriate punishment" can be made in each particular case.... Mental retardation is a factor that may well lessen a defendant's culpability for a capital offense. But we cannot conclude today that the Eighth Amendment precludes the execution of any mentally retarded person...convicted of a capital offense simply by virtue of their mental retardation alone."[58]

The debate over proportional penalties and torturous punishment was not argued in its fullest form in the death penalty cases. Instead, the Court used the case of convicted felon Jerry Helm from South Dakota to explore the relationship between crime and proportional punishment. In this 1983 case, *Solem v. Helm,* Mr. Justice Lewis F. Powell tied English constitutional documents to American law in a classic and landmark opinion. He began by restating the words of the Eighth Amendment to the U.S. Constitution and then immediately gave his conclusion in the following words: "The final clause [nor cruel and unusual punishments inflicted] prohibits *not only* barbaric punishments, *but also* sentences that are disproportionate to the crime committed."[59] Justice Powell did not find it necessary to document the belief that the cruel and unusual punishments provision prohibited barbaric methods. In fact, he noted that it was quite possible that the English Bill of Rights had not intended to prohibit use of barbaric methods. However, if this were so, then the American framers of the Eighth Amendment "may have intended the Eighth Amendment to go beyond the scope of its English counterpart...." Powell implied that he thought the framers had. Even Chief Justice Burger, in his dissenting opinion, was sure that the American framers had intended to prohibit inhumane methods of inflicting punishment and death. The Chief Justice said, "The framers viewed the Cruel and Unusual Punishment Clause as prohibiting the kind of torture meted out during the reign of the Stuarts." Burger noted that during the reign of the Stuarts punishments and penalties had taken on aspects of torture. These were well known to the framers of the Eighth Amendment who wanted to prohibit such methods in the United States.

Justice Powell, however, moved beyond this to prove that English law had always operated under a doctrine of non-excessiveness and proportionality for determining sentences. He examined the provisions of Magna Carta devoted to proportional penalties and noted that this had been reaffirmed under Edward I in the First Statute of Westminster (1297). Powell also cited the English common law cases invalidating disproportionate punishments: *Le Gras v. Bailiff of Bishop of Winchester*, (1316) and *Hodges v. Humkin*, (1615). He highlighted the latter case precedent because it dealt with prison sentences, the exact issue before the U.S. Supreme Court in *Helm. Hodges* showed that "the common law principle [of proportional punishment] incorporated into the Eighth Amendment clearly applied to prison terms." Prison sentences had been subjected to proportionality analysis from these early times, and judges were expected to decide whether the length and type of sentence was appropriate punishment for the crime committed, or whether it was excessive.

Thus Justice Powell and the majority of the court could conclude that in England from 1215–1615 the concept that punishment must be proportional to the crime was firmly held among Englishmen. Was this concept inherent in the English Bill of Rights (1689)? Powell stated his view thus: "The English Bill of Rights repeated the principle of proportionality...." His historical basis for this linkage came from the *Earl of Devon's Case* (1689), the proportionality case decided soon after the passage of the English Bill of Rights.

Powell's second and third areas of inquiry focused on the original intent of the American framers of the Eighth Amendment. He held that, "when the Framers of the Eighth Amendment adopted the language of the English Bill of Rights, they also adopted the English principle of proportionality." Powell noted that colonial Americans had always demanded "all the benefits secured to the subject by the English constitution," and he concluded that if Englishmen had proportional punishment in England then Americans would assume that they were entitled to it also. In Powell's view, "the Framers [of the Eighth Amendment] . . . intended to provide at least the same protection—including the right to be free from excessive punishments." The U.S. Supreme Court then concluded that Jerry Helm's sentence of life imprisonment for relatively minor criminal conduct was a "sentence . . . significantly disproportionate to his crime, and . . . therefore prohibited by the Eighth Amendment."[60] Thus *Titus Oates* came of age.

While American courts would refuse to find the death penalty a *per se* violation of the Eighth Amendment's cruel and unusual punishment prohibition, they would, nevertheless, outlaw penalties that were torturous and also insist on proportional punishment. Choosing not to follow the evolving standards that in England by the twentieth century had led to the abandonment of the death penalty, American judges nevertheless found English constitutional documents and legal history to be useful in giving meaning to the U.S. Bill of Rights' Eighth Amendment. Thus the ancient concepts of proportionality and the role of judges in evaluating sentences would work to keep the American legal system alert to miscarriages of justice.

NOTES

1. The Trial of Titus Oates, D.D. for Perjury, 1685, T. B. Howell, ed., *State Trials* (London: 1816–1828), vol. 10, pp. 1,079–330.

2. Solem v. Helm, 463 U.S. 277 (1983).

3. The Trial of Titus Oates, Howell, *State Trials*, vol. 10, pp. 1,314–325.

4. Ibid., p. 1,325. See also Elaine Kidner Dakers, *Titus Oates* (Westport, CT: Greenwood Press, 1971), p. 319.

5. Solem v. Helm, 463 U.S. 277 (1983).

6. Ibid.

7. Ibid., p. 303.

8. Leon Radzinowicz, *A History of English Criminal Law and Its Administration From 1750,* vol. 1 (London: Stevens and Sons, Ltd., 1948), p. ix.

9. Ibid., pp. 23–28.

10. G. O. Sayles, *The Medieval Foundations of England,* 2d ed. (London: Methuen & Co., 1964) pp. 232–34.

11. A. E. Dick Howard, *The Road From Runnymede: Magna Carta and Constitutionalism in America* (Charlottesville: University Press of Virginia, 1968), pp. 6–8.

12. Anthony F. Granucci, "Nor Cruel and Unusual Punishments Inflicted: The Original Meaning," 57 *California Law Review* (1969), pp. 839, 846.

13. David L. Keir, *The Constitutional History of Modern Britain Since 1485,* 8th ed. (Princeton, NJ: Van Nostrand, 1966), pp. 129–30.

14. See *Hodges v. Humkin,* E. Bulstrode, *The Reports of Edward Bulstrode:...In Three Parts...of Cases in Kings Bench, 1609–29,* 2nd ed. (London: 1688), Part 2, pp. 139–40.

15. Irving Brant, *The Bill of Rights* (New York: Mentor Books, 1967), pp. 134–66.

16. James Heath, *Torture and English Law: An Administrative and Legal History from the Plantagenets to the Stuarts* (Westport, CT: Greenwood Press, 1982), pp. 74–142.

17. Richard L. Perry, ed., *Sources of Our Liberties* (Chicago, IL: American Bar Foundation, 1959), p. 312.

18. Ibid.

19. Robin Clifton, *The Last Popular Rebellion: The Western Rising of 1685* (New York: St. Martin's, 1984), pp. 231–43. See also David Ogg, *England In the Reigns of James II and William III* (Oxford: The Clarendon Press, 1955), pp. 149–54.

20. J. Elliot, *The Debates in the Several States on the Adoption of the Federal Constitution* 111, 2d. ed. (1881), pp. 447–48.

21. Brant, *The Bill of Rights,* p. 71. See also 1 *Annals of Congress* (1789), pp. 782–83.

22. *Congressional Globe,* 39th Congress, 1st Session, 2,542.

23. Frederick Pollock and F. W. Maitland, The *History of English Law,* vol. 1 (Cambridge: Cambridge University Press, 1978), pp. 174–78, 183–84, 200–2, 224.

24. Ibid., vol. 2., pp. 467–70, 670–71, 674. See also J. Stephen, *History of the Criminal Law of England,* vol. 3, (London: Macmillan, 1883), pp. 44, 46, 73.

25. Le Gras v. Bailiff of Bishop of Winchester, 10 Edward II (1316).

26. Hodges v. Humkin, Bulstrode, *Reports,* vol. 2, pp. 139, 140.

27. Ibid.

28. Howell, ed., *State Trials,* vol. 10, p. 1,314.

29. Ibid.

30. Wilkerson v. Utah, 99 U.S. 130 (1879).

31. O'Neil v. Vermont, 144 U.S. 323 (1892).

32. Ibid.

33. Howell, ed., *State Trials,* vol. 10, p. 1,314.

34. A. V. Dicey, *Introduction to the Study of the Law of the Constitution,* 10th ed. (London: Macmillan/St. Martin's Press, 1973), pp. 43, 43, 48.

35. William Blackstone, *Commentaries on the Laws of England* vol. 1 (Birmingham, AL: Gryphon Legal Classics, 1983), p. 156.

36. Sir Edward Coke, *The Reports of Sir Edward Coke, Knt., in English in Thirteen Parts Complete* vol. 8, (Dublin, 1793), pp. 107, 118.

37. Howell, ed., *State Trials,* vol. 10, p. 1,314.

38. Stanford v. Kentucky, 492 U.S. 361 (1989).

39. Ibid.

40. Hodges v. Humkin, Bulstrode, *Reports,* vol. 2, p. 139 (1615).

41. 217 U.S. 349 (1910).

42. Richard L. Perry, *Sources of our Liberties,* pp. 65–66, 70, 75, 101–4, and 330–66. See also William S. Holdsworth, *A History of English Law,* vol. 9 (Boston: Little, Brown, 1937), pp. 108–17.

43. McGautha v. California, 402 U.S. 350 (1971).

44. Earl of Devon's Case, Howell, ed., *State Trials,* vol. 11, p. 1,354.

45. O'Neil v. Vermont, 144 U.S. 323 (1892).

46. Weems v. United States, 217 U.S. 349 (1910).

47. Ibid., p. 367.

48. Granucci, "Nor Cruel and Unusual Punishments Inflicted," p. 859.

49. 408 U.S. 238, 336–38 (1972).

50. Ibid., p. 319.

51. Stanford v. Kentucky, 492 U.S. 361 (1989) and Wilkins v. Missouri, 482 U.S. 361 (1989).

52. Thompson v. Oklahoma 487 U.S. 815 (1988).

53. Penry v. Lynaugh, 492 U.S. 302 (1989).

54. Ford v. Wainwright 477 U.S. 399 (1986).

55. Penry v. Lynaugh, 492 U.S. 302 (1989).

56. See Chapter 4 of this text.

57. Penry v. Lynaugh, 492 U.S. 302 (1989).

58. Ibid.

59. Solem v. Helm, 463 U.S. 277 (1983).

60. Ibid.

Epilogue

Litigation is a process deeply rooted in America: "The United States was founded on law and on a legal system that centered on litigation."[1] That moral issues are debated within this system is not, therefore, surprising. Law itself documents the moral choices of past and present generations while the legal process operates to test the scope and limits of the law. Thus moral issues can be understood in part by understanding the legal process as it has operated historically to manage the conflicting societal views and demands. This American legal process is, as we have seen, an inherited English process: The English legal system served to teach and educate Americans in using litigation to manage conflicts. The legal framework's component parts evolved from English practices to develop in the American environment. American decision makers from earliest times appealed to English traditions and processes to find sources for the moral values they adopted. English legal history has thus provided both inspiration and justification for American policy makers dealing with moral questions. The roles played by English scholars and attorneys; by English statutory laws and constitutional documents; and by English judicial traditions are useful factors as moral issues are litigated within the American legal framework.

The fact that the moral questions themselves are not definitively settled does not reflect negatively on the process itself. Instead, the value of litigation lies in its framework within which debates over irreconcilable moral positions can take place in an orderly and reasoned fashion. Moreover, the framework's parts have individually and collectively influenced the course of moral disputes. Thus, abortion questions have been impacted not only by legal scholars and authorities, but by all of the elements of the legal process. Attorneys like Sara Weddington and Frank Susman helped set the parameters of the debate. The abortion statutes tested were the products of state legislative actions from the 1820s through the 1980s. And in the absence of specific constitutional statements about abortion, justices like Harry A. Blackmun, Antonin E. Scalia, and Chief Justice William H. Rehnquist fulfilled the same historic judicial function performed by English predecessors like Sir Matthew Hale—creating and applying judicial tests.

Sodomy questions, too, have been influenced by all of the elements of the legal process. Sodomy statutes enacted by the sixteenth-century's Henry VIII and by the twentieth-century's Georgia legislature are not sufficient alone for understanding this moral debate. As statutes about sodomy were drafted and then involved in litigation, other parts of the legal process came into play. The litigation of this moral issue has demonstrated that legal authorities like Coke and Blackstone were cited continuously. Attorneys like Laurence H. Tribe developed significant litigation strategies and arguments. And in the absence of clear constitutional statements, jurists like Byron R. White, Lewis F. Powell, and Harry A. Blackmun moved to develop judicial tests.

Judicial tests for defining pornography have moved from the early English "Hicklin" test to the contemporary American "Miller" test. These tests were products of the total legal process at work. Attorneys like Charles Rembar developed, for example, historical arguments that affected the litigation over pornography/obscenity. Legislative statutes whether couched in the terms of Lord Campbell's Act (1857) or those of a U.S. Congress in the Comstock Act (1873) set the stage for litigation involving pornography. Ultimately many legislative bodies would write statutes based on the judicial tests, thus bringing the legal process to full circle. The absence of historic scholarly treaties coupled with specific constitutional grants of free speech helped produce debates which could be managed only through the device of judicial tests.

The definition of criminal insanity and the parameters of the insanity plea have been especially altered by attorneys, but other parts of the legal process have also exercised significant influence. Judges have acted with wide discretion, devising tests, from the "wild beast" test through "irresistible impulse" to "diminished responsibility." They have tried to mediate the interaction of the legal process with modern medical science as attorneys introduced expert witnesses. Constitutional provisions have offered little guidance apart from occasional efforts to apply the prohibitions against cruel and unusual punishment to verdicts in insanity cases. Legal authorities have proven most useful to the courts from Bracton and Hale to the American Legal Institute's Model Code, yet neither the accumulation of authoritative opinion and precedent, nor the rise of psychiatry and psychology have made possible any easy application in insanity cases. Statutes have done little more than record established precedent and prevailing opinion belatedly, and usually in response to some sensational case. The limited role played by constitutional provisions and statutes has left a wider area for the other elements to influence the process—attorneys, judicial tests, legal authorities—and indeed they have on both sides of the Atlantic.

The Constitution's prohibition of cruel and unusual punishment did not settle disputes about the death penalty or proportionate punishments. Even when coupled with its historic predecessor, the English Bill of Rights of 1689, the meaning of the provision has remained open to debate. Appeals to scholars and authorities like Blackstone generated partial answers. Statutory laws as old as the Anglo-Saxon dooms and as modern as the Federal Anti-Drug Abuse Act of 1988 document society's evolving standards. And, finally, judicial tests from seventeenth-century English cases like *Titus Oates* to twentieth-century American cases like *Weems* (1910), *Furman* (1972), and *Helm* (1983), have developed and given meaning to the constitutional provision.

Appeal to such factors may document a deliberate rationalization used by American legal decision makers to express sharply divergent personal policy predilections.[2] It may, on the other hand, demonstrate the socializing influence of traditional legal modes or "categories of discourse"[3] on these decision makers. In any case, the resort to an historic legal process for debate over continuing moral controversies demonstrates that "policy makers live in history whether they want to or not; and they can't help appealing to history for inspiration or justification."[4] Decision makers continually mine the past to find traditions and sources of moral values for justifying or criticizing current policies. Legal history in providing the tie to the past reaches also to the future to serve current political and jurisprudential aims.

NOTES

1. Jethro K. Liebermen, *The Litigious Society* (New York: Basic Books, 1981), p. 15.
2. Robert W. Gordon and William Nelson, "An Exchange on Critical Legal Studies," 6 *Law and History Review* (Spring 1988), pp. 139–86. See p. 145.
3. Ibid., p. 171.
4. Ibid., p. 141.

Bibliography

BOOKS

Acts and laws, passed by the great and general council of assembly of the province of Massachusetts Bay in New England from 1692 to 1719. London: J. Bashelt, 1724.

Bailey, D. S. *Homosexuality in the Western Christian Tradition*. Hamden, CT: Archon, 1975.

Blackstone, William. *Commentaries on the Laws of England*. Birmingham, AL: Gryphon Legal Classics Library Edition, 1983.

Boswell, John. *Christianity, Social Tolerance, and Homosexuality*. Chicago: University of Chicago Press, 1980.

Bowen, Catherine. *The Lion and the Throne: The Life and Times of Sir Edward Coke*. Boston: Little, Brown, 1956.

Boyer, Paul S. *Purity in Print: The Vice Society Movement and Book Censorship in America*. New York: Charles Scribner's Sons, 1968.

Bracton, Henry de. *De Legibas et Consuetudinibus Angliae* (On the Laws and Customs of England), edited by George E. Woodbine, translated by Samuel E. Thorne. 4 vols. Cambridge MA: Belknap Press of Harvard, 1968–1977.

Bradford, William. *History of Plymouth Plantation, 2 Vols*. Boston: Houghton Mifflin, 1912.

Brant, Irving. *The Bill of Rights*. New York: Mentor Books, 1967.

Britton. Francis Nichols, ed. Oxford: Clarendon, 1865.

Bulstrode, E. *The Reports of Edward Bulstrode: . . . In Three Parts . . . of Cases in Kings Bench. 1609–29*. London, 1688.

Caplan, Lincoln. *The Insanity Defense and the Trial of John W. Hinckley, Jr.* Boston: Godine, 1984.

Carrington, F. A., and J. Payne. *Reports of Cases Argued at Nisi Prius*. London: Sweet, 1825–1891.

Clifton, Robin. *The Last Popular Rebellion: The Western Rising of 1685*. New York: St. Martin's, 1984.

Cobbett, W., and T. Howell, eds. *Complete Collection of State Trials*. 33 vols. London, 1809–1826.

Coke, Edward. *The Third Part of the Institutes of the Laws of England*. London: E & R Brooke, 1797.

Collinson, George D. *A Treatise on the Law Concerning Idiots, Lunatics and Other Persons Non Compotes Mentis*. London: W. Reed, 1812.

Dakers, Elaine Kidner. *Titus Oates*. Westport, CT: Greenwood Press, 1971.

Dalton, Michael. *The Countrey Justice: Containing the Practice of the Justices of the Peace out of their Sessions*. New York: Arno Press Reprint, 1972.

Dicey, A. V. *Introduction to the Study of the Law of the Constitution*. London: Macmillan/St. Martin's Press, 1973.

Dictionary of National Biography. Leslie Stephen and Sidney Lee, eds. 66 vols. London: Oxford University Press, 1885–1901.

Elliott, J. *The Debates in the Several States on the Adoption of the Federal Constitution*. 1881.

Epstein, William H. *John Cleland: Images of a Life*. New York: Columbia University Press, 1974.

Fingarette, Herbert. *The Meaning of Criminal Insanity*. Berkeley: University of California Press, 1972.

Fingarette, Herbert, and Ann Fingarette Hasse. *Disabilities and Criminal Responsibility*. Berkeley: University of California Press, 1979.

Fleta. H. G. Richardson and G. O. Sayles, eds. London: Quaritch, 1955.

Garfield, Jay L., and Patricia Hennessey, eds. *Abortion: Moral and Legal Perspectives*. Amherst: The University of Massachusetts Press, 1984.

Goldstein, Abraham. *The Insanity Defense*. New Haven: Yale University Press, 1967.

Hale, Matthew. *History of the Pleas of the Crown*. 1736.

Hansard Parliamentary Debates, 3d Series. 1857.

Hanson, Laurence. *Government and the Press*. Oxford: Clarendon Press, 1936; reprint 1967.

Hawkins, William. *Treatise of the Pleas of the Crown*. 1716.

Hawley, J., and M. McGregor. *The Criminal Law*. 1899.

Heath, James. *Torture and English Law: An Administrative and Legal History from the Plantagenets to the Stuarts*. Westport, CT: Greenwood Press, 1982.

Holdsworth, W. S. *The Historians of Anglo-American Law*. Hamden, CT: Archon Books, 1966.

———. *A History of English Law*. 13 vols. Boston: Little, Brown, 1937.

Howard, A. E. Dick. *The Road From Runnymede: Magna Carta and Constitutionalism in America*. Charlottesville: University Press of Virginia, 1968.

Huser, Roger J. *The Crime of Abortion in Canon Law*. Washington, DC: The Catholic University of America Press, 1942.

Hyde, H. Montgomery. *A History of Pornography*. London: Heinemann, 1964.

———. *The Love That Dared Not Speak Its Name: A Candid History of Homosexuality in Britain*. Boston: Little, Brown, 1970.

Irons, Peter. *The Courage of Their Convictions*. New York: Penguin, 1990.

Keir, David L. *The Constitutional History of Modern Britain Since 1485*. Princeton, NJ: Van Nostrand, 1966.

Keown, John. *Abortion, Doctors and the Law*. New York: Cambridge University Press, 1988.

Lambarde, William. *Eirenarcha, or Of the Office of the Justices of Peace*. London, 1610.

Landmark Briefs and Argument of the Supreme Court of the United States: Constitutional Law. Vol 75. Philip B. Kurland and Gerhard Casper, eds. Arlington, VA: University Publications of America, 1975.

Lewis, Felice F. *Literature, Obscenity and Law*. Carbondale and Edwardsville: Southern Illinois University Press, 1976.

Liebermen, Jethro. *The Litigious Society*. New York: Basic Books, 1981.

Loth, David. *The Erotic in Literature*. London: Secker and Warburg, 1961.

Maitland, F. W. *Select Pleas of the Crown*. London: Quaritch, 1888.

Mitchell, J. T., and H. Flanders, eds. *The statutes at large of Pennsylvania from 1682 to 1801*. Harrisburg: Clarence Busch, 1896.

Mohr, James C. *Abortion in America: The Origin and Evolution of National Policy, 1800–1900*. New York: Oxford University Press, 1978.

Moore, Michael S. *Law and Psychiatry: Rethinking the Relationships*. Cambridge, MA: Cambridge University Press, 1984.

Moran, Richard. *Knowing Right from Wrong: The Insanity Defense of Daniel Mc-Naughton*. New York: The Free Press, 1981.

Morton, Thomas. *The History of the Pennsylvania Hospital, 1751–1895*. Philadelphia: Times Printing House, 1897.

Noonan, John T., Jr., ed. *The Morality of Abortion: Legal and Historical Perspectives*. Cambridge, MA: Harvard University Press, 1970.

Ogg, David. *England in the Reigns of James II and William III*. Oxford: The Clarendon Press, 1955.

Perry, Richard L., ed. *Sources of Our Liberties*. Chicago, IL: American Bar Foundation, 1959.

Peskin, Allen. *Garfield: A Biography*. Kent, OH: Kent State University Press, 1978.

Phelps, Glenn A., and Robert A. Poirier, eds. *Contemporary Debates on Civil Liberties: Enduring Constitutional Questions*. Lexington, MA: D. C. Heath and Co., 1985.

Pollock, Frederick, and Maitland, F. W. *The History of English Law before the Time of Edward I*. Cambridge: Cambridge University Press, 1895, new ed. 1968.

Radzinowicz, Leon. *A History of English Criminal Law and Its Administration From 1750*. London: Stevens and Sons, 1948.

Ray, Isaac. *A Treatise on the Medical Jurisprudence of Insanity*. Boston: Little, Brown, 1838; Belknap Press, 1962.

Rembar, Charles. *The End of Obscenity: The Trials of Lady Chatterly, Tropic of Cancer, and Fanny Hill*. New York: Random House, 1968.

Rosenberg, Charles E. *The Trial of the Assassin Guiteau: Psychiatry and Law in the Gilded Age*. Chicago: University of Chicago Press, 1968.

Sayles, G. O. *The Medieval Foundations of England*. London: Methuen and Co., 1964.

St. John-Stevas, Norman. *Obscenity and the Law*. London: Secker and Warburg, 1956.

Select Trials at the Sessions-House in the Old Bailey, 1720–1742. London: Applebee, 1742; Garland-Publishing Co. Reprint 1985.

Siebert, Frederick S. *Freedom of the Press in England, 1476–1776: The Rise and Decline of Government Control.* Urbana: University of Illinois Press, 1965.

Simon, Rita J., and David E. Aaronson. *The Insanity Defense: A Critical Assessment of Law and Policy in the Post-Hinckley Era.* New York: Praeger, 1988.

Staples, W. R., ed. *Proceedings of the first general assembly of the incorporation of Providence Plantation and the code of laws adopted in 1647.* Providence: Charles Bunett, 1847.

Staughton, G., et. al. *Charter of William Penn and Laws of the Commonwealth of Pennsylvania . . . preceded by Duke of York's laws.* Harrisburg: Lane S. Hart, 1879.

Stephen, Sir James F. *History of the Criminal Law of England.* London: Macmillan, 1883.

Straus, Ralph. *The Unspeakable Curll: Being Some Account of Edmund Curll, Bookseller, to Which is Added a Full List of His Books.* London: Chapman and Hall, 1927.

Sutherland, John. *Offensive Literature: Decensorship in Britain 1960–1982.* Totowa, NJ: Barnes and Noble Books, 1982.

Szaz, Thomas, ed. *The Age of Madness: The History of Involuntary Mental Hospitalization Presented in Selected Texts.* Garden City, NY: Doubleday, 1973.

Tatalovich, Raymond, and Byron Daynes, eds. *Social Regulatory Policy: Moral Controversies in American Politics.* Boulder, CO: Westview Press, 1988.

Tribe, David. *Questions of Censorship.* New York: St. Martin's Press, 1973.

Tribe, Laurence H. *American Constitutional Law.* Mineola, NY: The Foundation Press, 1978.

Tribe, Laurence, and Michael Dorf. *On Reading the Constitution.* Cambridge, MA: Harvard University Press, 1991.

Wade, E. C. S., and G. Godfrey Phillips. *Constitutional and Administrative Law.* New York: Longman, 1977.

Walker, Nigel. *Crime and Insanity in England.* Vol. 1, *The Historical Perspective.* Edinburgh: University Press, 1968.

Wertham, Fredric. *The Show of Violence.* New York: Doubleday, 1949.

West, Donald, and Alexander Walk, eds. *Daniel McNaughton: His Trial and the Aftermath.* Ashford, England: Headley Brothers, 1977.

Winslade, William, and Judith Ross. *The Insanity Plea.* New York: Charles Scribner's Sons, 1983.

Woodward, Bob, and Scott Armstrong. *The Brethren: Inside the Supreme Court.* New York: Simon & Schuster, 1979.

ARTICLES

Alpert, Leo M. "Judicial Censorship of Obscene Literature." 52 Harvard Law Review 40–43 (1938).

American Bar Association. *Report on Standings for Criminal Justice: Nonresponsibility for Crime.* Chicago: American Bar Association (1983).

American Law Institute. Model Penal Code, 4.01. Proposed Official Draft, 1962. See also Michael S. Moore, *Law and Psychiatry,* 219–222.

Bingham, Caroline. "Seventeenth-Century Attitudes Toward Deviant Sex." 1 *Journal of Interdisciplinary History.* 448–68 (Spring 1971).

Bowman, Karl M. "A Psychiatric Evaluation of Laws of Homosexuality." 29 *Temple Law Quarterly* 273–81 (1956).

Crompton, Louis. "Homosexuals and the Death Penalty in Colonial America." *Journal of Homosexuality,* vol. 1, 280–81 (1976).

Gordon Robert W., and William Nelson. "An Exchange on Critical Legal Studies." 6 *Law and History Review,* 139–86 (Spring 1988).

Granucci, Anthony F. "Nor Cruel and Unusual Punishments Inflicted: The Original Meaning." 57 *California Law Review* 839, 846 (1969).

"Hearings before the Subcommittee on Criminal Law of the Committee on the Judiciary, United States Senate, Ninety-Seventh Congress, Second Session," June 24, 30 and July 14, 1982. Washington, DC: U.S. Government, Printing Office, 1983.

Means, Cyril C., Jr. "The Law of New York Concerning Abortion and the Status of the Foetus." 14 *New York Law Forum* 418 (1968).

———. "The Phoenix of Abortional Freedom: Is a Penumbral or Ninth-Amendment Right About to Arise from the Nineteenth-Century Legislative Ashes of a Fourteenth Century Common Law Liberty." 17 *New York Law Forum* 385 (1971).

Morris, Norval. "Insanity Defense: The National Institute of Justice Crime File Study Guide." Washington, DC: U.S. Department of Justice, 1988.

Platt, Anthony M. "The Origins and Development of the 'Wild Beast' Concept of Mental Illness and Its Relation to Theories of Criminal Responsibility." *Issues in Criminology,* vol. 1, no. 1 (Fall 1965).

Platt, Anthony, and Bernard L. Diamond. "The Origins of the 'Right and Wrong' Test of Criminal Responsibility and Its Subsequent Development in the United States: An Historical Survey." 54 California Law Review, 1,250–58 (1966).

Rohrs, Richard C. "Partisan Politics and the Attempted Assassination of Andrew Jackson." 1 *Journal of the Early Republic,* 149–63 (1981).

Sayre, Francis B. "Mens Rea." 45 *Harvard Law Review,* 1,005–1,006 (1932).

Thompson, Ralph. "Deathless Lady." *The Colophon,* New Series, vol. 1, no. 2, 207–20 (1935).

"Transcripts of Arguments Before High Court on Abortion Case." *New York Times,* B12-B14 (1989).

Vail, R. W. G. "A Curtain Call for Benjamin Gomez." *The Colophon,* Part 9 (1939).

Index

About the Authors

WAYNE C. BARTEE is Professor of History at Southwest Missouri State University. He is the author of several books and articles in leading scholarly journals.

ALICE FLEETWOOD BARTEE is Professor of Political Science at Southwest Missouri State University. She is the author of *Cases Lost, Cases Won* and a contributor to *The Oxford Companion to the Supreme Court*.